"Self Portrait With Stubble"
from an oil painting by the author

When We Were Eagles

and

Other Stories

by

John Hawson

This edition published 2002

ISBN 0-9544195-0-2

Published by
Over Longtail Publishing,
Bowness on Windermere,
Cumbria, England LA23 3HU.

For Anne.

Contents.

When We Were Eagles.

It was a Friday evening. Bill McKerrow, David Nichols and I gathered in the car park of Aberdeen Royal Infirmary. We piled up our various rucksacks, tents, ropes, climbing and camping gear and threw them in the back of Bill's car.

Bill had, at that time, a maroon MGBGTV8. I had never known a car with so many letters. What's more, it had a power bulge on the bonnet, under which its huge engine was barely accommodated. Apparently the power bulge was an additional refinement seen only on a select few motors.

Bill liked his cars fast, and this one certainly was. Unfortunately its carrying capacity was not one of its noteworthy features and I found myself crammed into the back in a crouched position because the slope of the rear, with its tiny window, was more conducive to speed than to carrying tall passengers.

Integral to the car was its sound system which boasted several loudspeakers one of which was adjacent to my left ear: so we set off with the roar of the engine and the sound of John Denver reverberating around us…… "In Colorado Rocky Mountain high, I've seen it raining fire in the sky….." and "I am the eagle, I live in high places….." and when the tyres screeched as we rounded corners we screamed in unison, " We're all dooooomed!" with the sort of Scottish accent that Frazer (the undertaker in Dad's Army) used to have.

The year was 1974 and we were all young doctors, and bound for Torridon where David had selected the Central Buttress of Choire Mhic Fearchair for us to climb.

To the songs of John Denver we swung merrily along the roads as the late evening sun dipped into the Western sky, arriving with a crunch of gravel under the slopes of Liathach where we disembarked and put up the Vango Force Ten tent.

David had chosen this tent because, he explained, it had a midge-proof lining and a net filter which would allow us to breathe but not let the midges in.

The short night passed uneventfully but morning necessitated us leaving the tent and, of course, in came the midges. Within seconds we were inundated with the blighters. They were in our hair, up our noses, inhaled with every breath, and they sank their fangs into their favourite parts of our bodies – eyelids, earlobes, neck and wrists.

It was useless trying to cook or do anything other than flee the tent.

We ran for the car and slammed the doors shut hoping to escape the onslaught of the midges, but they got in through air vents and suchlike. The air inside our car was thick with them.

There was nothing for it but to put on our rucksacks and set off for the hills.

Choire Mhic Fhearchair is a dark, high, remote corrie on the North side of Beinn Eighe. To reach it we had to skirt between Liathach and Beinn Eighe along the valley floor. The walk was several miles long and we entertained ourselves listening to David as he told us about the latest book he was reading.

David was always entertaining us with tales. His knowledge was immense – either that, or he just made it up! But he knew exactly how many thousand impis (that's the name for Zulu warriors) were at the battle of Isandlwhana, for the book of the moment was called "The Washing of the Spears", an epic all about the Zulu wars and the defeat of the British army by Shaka Zulu and his troops at Isandlwhana.

So we heard what British regiments were there, what were their positions and arms and tactics, how many officers, and what their names were; but what I recall best was the bit about how the noise made by the 150,000 impis, when they all beat their shields with their spears and ululated, was so great that it could be heard 20 miles away. This noise struck fear into the heart of the British soldiers and though they fought bitterly they were overwhelmed to a man and impaled on assegais or beaten by knobkerries.

We were informed about every detail of the massive slaughter.

Thus the walk passed most enjoyably.

We would question David who would then enlarge with explicit and vivid answers so that we could visualise exactly what was going on in the battle.

We stopped at times to refresh ourselves with spring water which trickled from the slopes of Beinn Eighe to our right and it was good to drink.

David, as I recall, drank from a goblet that was made of concentric rings of pure silver, like bands, which, when pulled apart, interlocked forming a beaker which could then be compressed into a cluster of silver rings for ease of carrying. Apparently it had belonged to his grandfather and had seen service in the Afghan campaigns: anyhow it was a finer thing than anything Bill or I had.

We soon rounded the North Western boundary of the mountain and cut back into the dark corrie where the tarn lay, in whose waters were reflected the three buttresses of Choire Mhic Fearchair: Triple Buttress.

We made for the Central Buttress and, after scrambling up scree, were soon roping up at its foot.

We took it in turns to lead and it was a pleasant climb. The day was sunny and clear. It was the height of Summer and we rose out of the dark, cold shadows into the hot sunshine where the rock was warm to the touch.

The climbing was not too hard, but it is a remote corrie and is not to be underestimated.

As the day progressed, the space beneath our heels grew as we left pitch after pitch below.

If ever any one of us was having difficulty with a particular pitch the other two would spur him on with ululating noises and talk of assegais beating against shields, or occasionally giving a poke from below, or some sharp comment designed to induce more rapid movement – and, thus encouraged, the difficulties were more speedily overcome and we all moved upwards.

It was indeed a happy, carefree experience, and when we found ourselves sitting side by side on a narrow rock ledge, dangling our feet over the edge as we munched sandwiches, Bill remarked that this is exactly what eagles do – not munching sandwiches and dangling feet, of course, but sitting on a ledge peering out over the vast grandeur of the Scottish landscape.

It was an apposite remark and encapsulated the mood of the moment.

Later, when we had coiled the ropes at the top of the climb, we made the long descent over the summit of Beinn Eighe and back down to our little campsite……and the midges!

But the moment, and Bill's remark, and David's Zulu tales, and the echo of John Denver's songs still reminds me that it was a good time, for then we were eagles.

A Year In The Pfalz.

I stepped back from the Volkswagen camper van and admired my handiwork.

The old bus was painted a lurid shade of yellow, and, what's more, all the rusty bits were completely covered up!

Together Annie and I loaded up the ageing vehicle with all our possessions and set off from Aberdeen bound for Germany.

The road South from Dover through France took the best part of nine hours driving, and we passed through Luxembourg and

Saarbrücken before entering the wooded, hilly region which lies between the river Saar and the Rhein and which is known as the Rheinpfalz, but by this time it was dark and the rain was beginning to turn to sleet.

In the gloom, and with the windscreen wipers scraping away double time, we found our way through the industrial approaches of Pirmasens and up into the area where the vast complex of U.S. Army barracks was located, and then followed the directions we had for the village of Münchweiler where the 34th U.S. General Hospital was to be found.

The road out of Pirmasens dropped and twisted down the long, steep hill and then flattened out as it entered the valley floor.

All around there were signposts to little German villages leading off in various directions, but we followed the main road for several miles and then saw a sign for Münchweiler.

It had been a long journey and we were glad to be welcomed by Brian Baker, the commanding officer of the hospital where I was to work.

Brian was English, surprisingly, and a doctor, and he had joined the U.S. Army a few years before and had been posted out to Germany as had so many American soldiers.

This was 1976 and it was a dark November night.

The hospital was quite small and it served the soldiers and families of the entire U.S. army in that area – and there were many thousands of them.

It was an outpatient hospital and it had an accident department and an ambulance station. It had no beds for admitting patients, but it had close contact with the main U.S Army Hospital at Landstuhl, about twenty miles to the North.

There were a couple of career Army doctors in post, but the rest of the medical team were all civilians, like myself, who were either staying for a year or else on a permanent basis.

The first thing for Annie and myself to do was to find lodgings in the area and we were given a few names and addresses to check out.

It did not take us long to locate number 14, Langenbergstrasse in the village of Münchweiler, close by, and there we became tenants of Hubert and Rose Streb.

Hubert worked as a security guard on the main military base up in Pirmasens and he spoke excellent English; for all the world you would have taken him for an American!

They had two children and Oma, Hubert's elderly mother, and they all lived in the big house whilst we rented the apartment which was situated behind, in the garden.

We were very happy indeed.

Annie and I had been married only a short while and we both spoke German and got on very well with the Strebs who were kindness itself.

Across the village road was a little baker's shop and every

morning Annie or I would nip over and buy a brown paper bag with several fresh rolls – the ones we preferred were called brötchen mit Mohn, bread rolls with poppy seeds.

The American soldiers in Germany at that time were part of a vast army of occupation and their numbers had increased during the 'cold war' with Russia.

We were led to believe that the forests which covered thousands of square miles of that part of Germany were thick with concealed missile sites, and certainly the U.S. army was a very obvious presence in all the towns.

The young GIs seemed to have no interest in Europe. Their lives were totally wrapped up and catered for by the army. Their accommodation was military, the shops they visited were the American PX stores which were vast, duty-free shops dotted all over Germany, and they were allowed to buy duty-free cars to use whilst in Germany and to take home to America afterwards.

Even the petrol they bought was at a specially cheap price and available only for U.S. servicemen and to be found only at American duty-free petrol stations.

So all in all the American soldiers lived lives very much isolated from the German community in which they were posted.

Not so for us civilian doctors, however, because we had none of these duty-free privileges available to the American soldiers. Our lives were led very much as part of the local German neighbourhood even though we worked alongside all the enlisted men and the military doctors.

There was Kernel Dhillon. He was a Sikh with a black beard and a large turban. He was very smart and charming and he was one of the doctors on our team.

There was Steve McMillan, who was English and he was the civilian dentist looking after all the American teeth on the base.

Stuart Gadd was a young Australian doctor visiting Europe for a year. He started working in Münchweiler much the same time as I did and we became friends. He had bought himself a big, brand new BMW series '5' saloon having borrowed quite a lot of money, I believe, to do this, and his idea was to have a great time driving around most of Europe looking dead smooth in this luxury car and then transport it back to Australia and use it for a few years before selling it for twice what he had originally paid for it!

It all worked out exactly as he had planned – except for a few inconvenient incidents when he was crossing borders and had to get past efficient German border guards who doubtless thought, "Vy is zis scruffy young Australian driving vun of our glorious BMW autos? Perhaps he is a drug schmuggler? Ve vill arrest him and hav a leetle fun viz him. Ve vill ask him many qvestions und shine ze bright light in his face!" At any rate poor Stuart seemed to get stopped pretty often and after a weekend jaunt off to Switzerland or Berlin he would return looking a bit cheesed off having spent five hours driving and another five arguing his way out of a border police station.

Perhaps he would have been better off driving an old yellow van like mine!

Major Baker ran the show in a pleasant and orderly manner, and each day at the hospital would start off with us doctors seeing everybody who felt ill. There were lots of them!

The incidence of feeling ill increased dramatically whenever the troops were expected to do anything particularly physical.

One day the big chief General of all the U.S. forces in Europe sent round a message saying that he was coming round to check up on the state of fitness of everybody. He gave the date and time he intended to visit the 34th General Hospital (with approximately three months' notice) and he said that he expected all able-bodied soldiers to be able to run three miles in thirty minutes.

Now this same message went round Germany to all U.S. army units and cast fear into the hearts of all the commanding officers everywhere because it was well known that although the average GI may have been capable of smoking maybe twenty cigarettes in thirty minutes, or drinking several cans of Budweiser in that time, it was a bit much to expect them to do all this running.

So there came a cascade of orders emanating down from Major Baker through all the various ranks down to the staff sergeants whose job it was to ensure that all the men could do the run which the general required them to do.

I was in the clinic one afternoon and I could hear the pounding of booted feet on tarmac outside the window to the accompaniment of those squad training songs which you sometimes encounter if you watch army films or TV documentaries of soldiers training, particularly the U.S. military; you know what I mean – the sergeant sings one line and all the troops respond with the next one.

It sounded very tough and macho.

However the next morning our clinic was inundated with an exceptionally large number of sick men, and their sergeant made a general complaint on their behalf; "These men are ill, doc. They can't run at all and they go bright red in the face and they're terribly short of breath. They must have high blood pressure or something."

So it fell to us doctors to check them out for illness, but the real problem was that they were all too heavy and were in the habit of indulging in too much food and beer as well as cigarettes, and were definitely not in the habit of running.

Unfortunately there were a lot of them and no commanding officer wanted to be harangued by the big general for having the greatest number of unfit men in Europe, so a plan was hatched.

Training would be carried out fairly stringently, but if possible without inducing heart attacks in all the red-faced, breathless men,

and as the day of the general's visit approached 'profiles' would be given to all the sick men who were unable to do the three miles in thirty minutes and these profiles would excuse those men from having to run.

The end result was that when the general came he was delighted to see men running around the hospital and singing their army chants, and not one of them dropped out, so he gave us all very good marks!

Brian Baker was pleased!

What the general did not see, of course, were the dozens of overweight, red-faced and breathless men who would have shamed the whole unit had they been forced to perform.

Profiles are large sheets of paper issued by doctors within the U.S. military for the purpose of excusing the person from doing some specific physical activity,

For example a 'back profile' might be issued for a soldier with back pain. It would require the doctor to state specifically what is the maximum weight that man can lift, up to what height, and to be held there for how long, and whether he can push or pull what weight. The sergeants were always on the lookout for malingerers and would be careful to follow the profile up to its limit.

If, for example, lifting twenty pounds for two minutes to a height of three feet caused problems one would have to rewrite the whole profile to a lower requirement.

They were fairly voluminous documents so one tried to get it right first time!

Shaving profiles were the most commonly required because a troublesome shaving rash was quite common particularly with coloured men. We would then write a profile permitting the soldier to stop shaving for, say, fourteen days, and during that time to keep his beard trimmed to a length of no more than 4 mm.

It amused me to think of sergeants going round with a small ruler to make such exact measurements!

In the Winter Annie and I took the yellow peril to Grindlewald for some skiing. We prepared a large tub of stew to see us through a few days and this was kept cold although we had no fridge, for the van was itself a giant fridge.

Temperatures were far below zero all the time, and particularly so at night.

We slept in the camper van at Grindlewald, well wrapped up in our sleeping bags, and in the morning there would be a thick layer of frost all over the inside of the van.

The large tub of stew was a good idea in principle, but in practice the problem was that it remained frozen solid all the time, so we had to hack bits from it with a pocket knife and then heat them up in a smaller pan on the stove.

Annie endured the experience with good humour!

We skied the slopes below the Eiger and it was impressive to look up at its North Face above us.

On the way back home to Münchweiler we had several hours of motorway driving and this was where we really became aware of the shortcomings of the VW heating system, for the engine was air-cooled and located at the rear, so the pipe which was supposed to carry the heat up to the front of the van had several metres to travel, and the air was stone cold long before the halfway point.

Snow fell heavily all the way home and the windscreen kept getting obscured.

Annie reminds me that we stopped hundreds of times, every couple of miles, to scrape the windscreen, but I have forgotten such details!

One Winter's night, Brian Baker was away for a while and he had asked Annie and me to look after their cats.

It was early in the evening, pitch black, and it was snowing heavily.

The two of us set off in our yellow van and were driving the several miles to the Baker's home when in front of us on the road we saw a cluster of figures who appeared to be shining torches at us, and there was a police car parked by the side of the road.

We pulled over to where they were. We could see that they were German police officers and several of them were clicking their Schmeisser machine guns in what I thought was an unnecessary and rather threatening manner.

Their leader, a tall, thin man clad in high boots and a very long leather coat and with the sort of official hat on his head that I imagined a Gestapo officer might have worn, stepped forward and snapped some questions at us in staccato German.

"Who are you? Vy are you here? Vot are you doing? Vere are you going? Vot haf you got in your car?" and this sort of thing.

Obviously these were not his exact words because he spoke in German, but the translation would lose authenticity if it were expressed differently.

Annie and I stood there in the dark and with the snow falling heavily, and we were attempting to give a coherent reply when all of a sudden the officer snapped his fingers, uttered a guttural command and a large, heavy, uniformed man advanced towards our van, obviously intending to enter it.

He grabbed the sliding side-door and gave it a wrench, whereupon the door detached itself from the car and fell to the ground. It was not used to being so roughly handled. Some vital particle of rust had at last given way.

"Hi you!" I shouted - or it might even have been stronger than that - at any rate I was cross at seeing our camper van being demolished in front of our very eyes, and I began shouting back at them, notwithstanding the torchlight in our eyes.

To our amazement this had a dramatic effect.

The huge brute, who had inadvertently pulled the door off,

started to apologise abjectly, and the Gestapo officer retreated a couple of feet and looked a bit sheepish.

Annie stepped in at this point and with her immaculate German and calming manner she soon had us all good friends, at least the agreement was that we should carry on our way to feed the Baker's cats, and then the next day we should visit the police at their police station for further discussions.

A long piece of string was found and with polite if insincere chuckles it was tied all round the vehicle so as to hold the door in position.

Later that night, back in our apartment, we related this story to Hubert.

"Ah," he said, "You must go over the road and speak to Berndt. He will advise you."

So we did.

It turned out that Berndt, whom we had not met before, was himself a police officer and knew all about this police operation.

Apparently it was a drug snatch team and they were looking for drug smugglers.

When we described the various officers and men we had encountered he laughed uproariously; "Ho ho ho! Zat vould be Fritz. He is a good friend of mine. And ze big one, he is Hans. He is very strong, but clumsy! Come now, ve must haf some schnapps and get to know vun another."

And so we did.

Berndt explained that in Germany, even though we may not have been drug smugglers, there were some police officers who might consider it unsafe for a van to have a door which falls off so easily.

He advised us to give his compliments to the commanding officer and to assure them all that we would promptly have the little bit of rust replaced with a brand new metal part.

Perhaps it might be wise, he suggested with a chuckle, to replace all the rusty parts with, (polite cough), a newer car.

"Now my friends, another schnapps?"

At weekends Annie and I explored the woods in the Pfalz.

When Spring came I met some of the local climbing fraternity. They called themselves the PKV, the Pfälzer Kletterer Verein, which means the Pfalz climbing club.

They were a terrific bunch and we had a great deal of fun with them.

There was Uwe, who worked in Stuttgart during the week but who climbed almost nonstop each weekend. He was tall, agile, and a wonderfully aesthetic climber.

There was Heinz, who ran a pub called the Pilstube in Pirmasens during the week, and we often went back there to celebrate a good day's climbing.

Rolf was a very tall, immensely strong giant of a man. He was typically Prussian with a fiery temper and a thick moustache. He loved to pick fights whenever he could, particularly after a few beers and he was always plotting ambitious ascents of steep, hard routes.

Andreas was small and lithe and a very good climber indeed. His job was window-dressing for ladies' fashion shops. He had a big, bushy beard and lived about thirty miles away in one of the best wine-growing regions.

Theo was stocky and strong and had a wicked sense of humour but a tendency to become morose and easily upset. He loved the Pfalz with all his heart and hated any intruder who dared to set foot on "his" crags. Woe betide anyone who climbed using chalk to improve hand-grip on the rock, for if ever Theo found traces of chalk he would let loose with a torrent of invective which usually began with, "Scheisse! Mensch! Wahnsinn!" and went on to worse! These tirades could go on for ages.

I often went out climbing with Theo and I might be humming a happy tune as we walked through the woods in search of some climbing. Theo however would be frowning and cursing.

I would remark on how beautiful the woods were and how fresh and clean was the air, and I would ask Theo what could possibly be upsetting him, but this would elicit the response, "Scheisse! Mensch! Wahnsinn! Alle die Bäume sterben, Dschonn." - (that was my name – John!). He would explain that all the trees are dying, the air is poisoned, and the woods will soon be no more.

This rather cast a pall on things for a while, but he would perk up enormously when we rose up above the trees onto the top of some pillar, especially if the ascent had caused difficulty for me!

There was Peter Lischer, who had a climbing shop in Busenberg, a pretty village. He was a professional climber. He was immensely strong and knew every climb on every rock.

There was Walter (pronounced Valter) who was a photographer in Pirmasens, and there was Thomas who was at that time a student but who later went on to become a businessman in the shoe industry.

The whole of that region was famed for its shoe factories.

Off we would go at weekends along with our various wives and girlfriends and a cluster of dogs.

The climbing was on sandstone cliffs which were, by and large, concealed from view deep in the wooded hillsides. There are scores of such cliffs in the area and some are visible from the road, but most are not. So dense are the woods that sometimes you would be walking along, chatting, and suddenly you would bump your nose on a great sandstone tower that you had not noticed.

The sandstone crags were mostly vertical pillars rising up from the forest so the climbs were all pretty steep, and sandstone, being soft and easily eroded, did not readily lend itself to the placement of protection. The well-known climbing routes all had secure rings or pitons cemented into place, but not too frequently!

Very often a climb would be terrifically steep and with rounded, barely adequate holds or deep clefts in the rock, and you would climb higher and higher, and then would come the awful realisation that you were a long way above the last piece of protection, when mercifully you would come across a ring-peg and be able to clip into it and breathe more easily.

On the top of each pillar there is a large steel ring cemented into place, usually on the very edge of the cliff or at an overhanging point, and from this ring we would make an abseil descent.

It was always, for me, a nervous moment to launch myself over the lip and lower myself down on a descendeur, passing first through space, then through the highest branches of trees, and finally onto solid ground below.

But the German lads were so skilled and familiar with these crags that they would leap over the edge with a whoop and a yell, with the rope intricately wrapped around their bodies in a classic abseil, taking two or three great bounds and springing themselves from the rock into space as they fell swiftly to earth.

These lads knew where all the pitons were, and they had in fact placed many of them themselves.

Of the various dogs which accompanied us Rolf's dog, especially, comes to mind.

It was a small terrier and would trot alongside us as we wandered through the woods in search of crags to climb. It had a fierce reputation, like its owner, and Rolf and his dog shared many similar personality traits.

When Rolf was in a good mood, so was his dog. But when Rolf was angry, which was quite frequently, he would shout and rage at the dog; "Du böse Hund! Beiss den Theo!" which being interpreted means, "Oh you wicked dog! Bite Theo!"

Whereupon the little terrier would pursue Theo, nipping his heels and even trying to sink his fangs into Theo's legs, causing Theo to run very fast indeed, to the amusement of all who were not being chased.

I took care to try to stay on the good side of Rolf and his böse Hund!

Another climber who came to join us on several occasions was Craig.

He was a U.S. jetfighter pilot and he flew F16s.

These planes tore across the sky over the Rheinpfalz, breaking the sound barrier, and rolling over in the sky and generally making a super racket. It must have been colossal fun for their pilots, and here was a real one. He sported a jaunty moustache and had a huge smile full of perfect white teeth.

The Germans always had difficulty pronouncing his name, which came out something like 'Krekk' – so that's what we called him!

We spent many weekends walking into the woods and then shinning up rock climbs in this most beautiful of areas.

On top of each rock pinnacle is a little metal box with a lid. When you have done a climb you write your name, and the date and the name of the route you have just climbed, into the little book which is kept in the box, using the pencil provided.

We spent many happy days clambering up and down these crags, and although there may have been a few cloudy days I confess I remember only sunshine.

One weekend we all decided to visit the Windstein, an old ruined castle built into a crag and situated just across the border into France. It was only about twenty miles away, and we met up at the little inn there which was run by an elderly lady who was friendly with all these lads. She knew them all by name and she produced an excellent meal of flammkuchen – a speciality of Alsace, and which is like a very thin pizza with finely chopped onions and bacon on top, set in sour cream. Delicious!

After dinner and beer and songs everybody piled into the barn beside the inn and slept soundly.

In the Winter was a festival called Faschings.

This seemed to be a continuous round of parties which went on night after night for almost the entire Winter! One night there would be a Faschings party in one village, and the next night in another.

There were many dozens of little villages dotted amongst the hills so it appeared possible to join a party every night – at least that is what all the locals seemed to do! At every party there were familiar faces and they all knew how to have a good time with beer, wine (which was generally drunk in litre mugs) and much singing and dancing and roasting of sausages.

In the Autumn there were the wine and beer festivals – which were much the same as Faschings, really, and took place in most of the villages. At these there would be singing, dancing, oompah bands, and roasted sausages and pork, and beer and wine in litre mugs – in fact pretty well exactly the same as Faschings! Maybe it was all Faschings anyhow but they just forgot when to stop!

Once the PKV went to one such village weinfest. Everybody was there; all the wives, girlfriends and dogs.

It may have been in Birkweiler, or Busenberg, or Dahn – my memory is hazy – but I do remember the delicious taste of the new wines, of which there were several grape-varieties, sold in huge mugs. Soon people started singing and harmonising. And then it was not long after that before Rolf began thumping the table and gesticulating.

Uh oh! Watch out for his little dog!

But it was an arm wrestling match that he was calling for.

Ever willing to oblige, I offered my arm and Rolf crashed it triumphantly onto the table, gave a terrific shout, and everybody cheered and demanded more drink!

Next he demolished someone else, though I think he had more of a struggle with some of the Polish and Rumanian girlfriends who were pretty tough customers.

At last there was only Peter Lischer, and this was a contest of two giants.

Glasses shook. Beer spilled. The table trembled. The onlookers trembled. The dogs barked and howled.

The shouts of the surrounding crowd rose to a crescendo which drowned even the oompah band, but sad to relate, my recollection is too hazy to announce what happened next!

In the Summer Annie and I were out walking one day when we stopped a stranger to ask for directions. We were in the vicinity of Lemberg castle, a ruin from the thirteenth century that was being rebuilt by a group of dedicated locals.

The man was called Rheinhold and this chance encounter grew into an enduring friendship.

He invited us into the castle where there was a bar with a number of people supping pea soup, drinking beer and generally making merry. This was the Pfälzer Wald Verein – the local walking club!

Rheinhold was the leader of this club and he was responsible, for very many years, for maintaining the trails, and their signs, which crisscross hundreds of kilometres of woods in that area.

Rheinhold worked for the local beer factory, Parkbräu, and you would have thought, to look at him, that he was their official beer-taster, but no, he was their delivery van driver, and a very popular man, of that you may have no doubt!

Together with Rheinhold and his wife Gisela and their PWV

friends we walked many days through their woods, often finding our way in and out of France, up and down hills and ruined castles, and certainly in and out of places where refreshment could be obtained – of which there were plenty.

The Autumn passed into Winter and the snow came again, bringing a Breughel-like touch to the landscape.

Castles and crags loomed up out of the mist and the fields lay white in the valleys.

Frost hung from the trees and rocks.

That Winter was our last in Germany, although we have returned many times since and have renewed acquaintance with Hubert and Rose, with Berndt, and with Theo, Uwe, Heinz, Thomas, Rheinhold and Gisela.

There is a hill overlooking Busenberg. It is called the Buhlstein.

It takes thirty minutes to walk up to the top of the fels and from there you can look South towards the Schloss Bewartstein, a mediaeval castle in the woods, and West over the pretty village of Schindhard towards Dahn.

You can see the Drachenfels rear up out of the trees near Busenberg, and the long valley to the East disappearing in the mist towards Bad Bergzabern.

An ocean of tree-clad hills extends before your eyes, standing like waves, fading into paler shades of blue in the distance.

Every Monday morning, very early, before he sets off for the long drive to the factory in Stuttgart for his working week, Uwe climbs, as he has done for many years, to the top of the Buhlstein and surveys the Pfalz.

A Hopeless Weekend.

I sat down for a moment, clinging to the steep undergrowth in the bush, finding it hard to keep from slipping downhill, so steep was the slope.

I found a clump of damp moss and sucked on it trying to extract some moisture, for I felt dehydrated. I wondered what I should do, or where I was.

I was completely lost.

At that moment the ground shook violently and kept on shaking for about twenty seconds.

"What the hell sort of country is this?" I thought, then laughed, because I could think of precious little else that could go wrong.

How had I got into this situation?

It started one Friday evening.

I had been in Picton, New Zealand, hardly long enough to get over my jet lag and had received an invitation to join two New Zealanders, Tom and John, from Blenheim, on a weekend trip to climb a 7,000 ft peak called Mt Hopeless in the Nelson Lakes National Park of South Island.

I drove to Blenheim to meet the other two, carrying with me what little I had in the way of equipment, for our luggage from England was not due to arrive for another couple of weeks. As I recall I had a pair of boots, socks, a pair of shorts, a thin jersey, and a headtorch and a rucksack. That was about it.

Seeing my pathetic selection of gear Tom threw a can of sardines and an apple at me, and as an afterthought a red plastic garment which might come in useful if it rained or got windy.

It was Summer in the South Island of New Zealand and the weather was hot.

Tom drove us to the Nelson Lakes Park which, to my surprise, was a drive of about three hours along mainly dirt roads. I knew nothing of our destination nor what lay in store for us. Tom had the map and I had glanced briefly at it, discerning that Mt Hopeless lay deep within the National Park, quite a few miles to the South of the road we were driving on. I was not sure of the scale, nor of our actual plans.

On arriving, we had to check into the park and tell the ranger where we were going, then John spoke to someone whom he knew and who was willing to drive us in his boat with outboard engine all the way down a lake, thereby saving us quite a few hours of walking through the bush.

I had been told that the bush was dense, but I was later to learn what that really meant.

At the South end of the lake we put on our headtorches for the sun had set during the hour's boat ride and it was pitch black.

I couldn't help noticing that John's headtorch was an acetylene one – of the type coalminers used to wear a century or more ago – containing a drip-feed of water onto some calcium carbide which caused a chemical reaction, and the acetylene gas thus produced was ignited with a match and burned in a polished brass cone that produced a weak beam of light.

We followed the flickering light of the acetylene lamp through marshy ground. I was wondering where we were bound for, and had presumed there would be a hut at the foot of the lake.

But not so; we tramped for quite a few hours, as I recall, fording several little rivers up to our thighs and negotiating several reed beds and marshy swamps.

Ever the acetylene light flickered onward.

It must have been midnight when we at last reached a wooden hut deep in the bush. It was very cold and I was done in partly from the unexpected length of the walk in to the hut and also partly from the lingering effects of jetlag, and not least because of the intense concentration required to follow the acetylene light through mile after mile of dense and difficult terrain in total darkness.

The two Kiwis seemed tough customers indeed and I felt I should acquit myself honourably and not appear too wimpish by saying something like "Thank God, we're here at last. What a long walk that was!" So instead I remarked glibly, " Are we stopping here for a minute?"

"Good idea mate," came the reply, "We'd reckoned on spending the night here because it's so steep up to the next hut. It's another 2,500ft to climb and it'll be hard in the dark because there's gonna be plenty ice about, but why don't we press on and get the bush behind us. We can make the high hut in two and a half to three hours."

Silently wishing I'd kept my mouth shut I followed, once again, the acetylene lamp.

This time it rose higher and higher in front of Tom and me as it bobbed about in the dense bush. The track was indeed steep and the higher we climbed the more ice was underfoot. It was steep enough to need hands for a pull-up much of the way.

I don't know what time we emerged above the bush, maybe 3.30 a.m., but above us was a clear, starry sky, and it was perishingly cold.

There appeared to be quite a lot of ice and snow about.

We bundled into the tiny tin hut which just allowed us to crouch inside and slept as best we could for maybe two or three hours till the sun hit the tin and we started to feel its heat.

I don't recall us eating or drinking much on that long night, and subsequently I was to regret this oversight.

We roped up outside the hut and made our way across snow and a boulder field to reach the foot of an imposing rock wall which rose not quite vertically above us.

For a few minutes we discussed who was going to lead, then I was volunteered on the basis that I had done more rock climbing than the other two.

So I led up the wall and although it was not too difficult, what struck me most was its instability. Virtually every other handhold would come away in my hand and I had to either put it carefully back in place or else lob it wide away from Tom and John below.

I think there must have been about three or four climbing pitches, perhaps 400 ft, before I hauled up onto the ridge and breathed a sigh of relief to get away from such dangerous and unstable a rock face.

When the three of us gathered on the ridge we spoke briefly of our plans but Tom and John were uncertain save that the summit must be considerably higher and to our right.

Clouds were gathering and it was already a lot colder.

Also up there on the ridge there was a wind.

Sometime after midday I became aware of my own tiredness, and at a notch in the ridge I decided to declare that I was loath to continue and that we should discuss plans – unless the summit was just a short way off.

It was not.

According to John there had to be at least another hour to go to the top, but he was not sure.

I was reluctant that the party should split, but I felt ill-prepared and ill-equipped for a climb that now seemed longer and harder than I had anticipated, and I felt it best to stay put, so I said that I intended to stop at the notch, and I wondered how the other two would respond.

"OK, mate," they said, "We'll press on to the top or as far as we can. You stay put and we'll meet you back here."

I suggested a time, 3 o'clock in the afternoon, and we agreed that we should meet at that time even if it meant the other two having to turn back before the summit.

Once I was on my own I listened to the increasing wind and it made a wailing, screeching sound as it tore across the mountain.

The clouds were gathering fast and it looked as if bad weather was coming.

Wearing merely shorts and a jersey I began to feel the cold.

As I stamped my feet and flapped my arms to try to keep warm I could hear the sound of rocks falling off the mountain.

They bounced and shattered with explosive noises, and, coupled with the screaming of the wind and the surrounding mist, my imagination began to play tricks on me and I was not sure if the sounds I had heard had been of rocks falling, or of my two companions as they fell to their deaths. It was hard to tell.

I opened my pack, got out the tin of sardines and the apple and ate them.

Three o'clock came and went. The clouds were now very thick and visibility was poor, down to a few yards.

I determined to wait another half hour.

By three thirty there was still no sign of my friends. I was getting really cold and the light was dimmer. A thick mist had descended on the mountain.

Had they fallen? Was it their cries and the sound of them falling that I had heard earlier? Or had it been merely a rock fall?

There was no way I could tell.

After waiting nearly an hour longer than we had agreed I decided to set off down, but I was loath to descend the loose rock wall on my own and with no rope, so I decided I had best keep to the ridge and try to work my way down in what I thought was the direction of the hut.

But direction was impossible to tell; the clouds were so thick and the wind was so strong that I felt an urgency to get down by whatever way was the easiest.

So I climbed down and down the ridge, able to see no more than a few metres in the thick cloud, and I tried to keep a sense of direction, but when I emerged below the thick layer of cloud which made a ceiling above my head I searched the landscape below me for any sign of the shiny tin hut – and there was none.

Before my eyes stretched a vast vista of endless trees going on for I didn't know how many miles. The light was very flat and it was getting near dusk and I found it hard to judge distance.

Far in the distance I glimpsed a shiny reflection of what might perhaps be a lake, but I was cold, tired, hungry and lost, and it was very many miles away and I could not be sure.

Below me I could see a stream and I decided to descend the mountainside to drink.

But I had misjudged the distance and what I had thought was a small stream only a short distance below me turned out to be quite a large river a few thousand feet below.

As I picked my way down the steep mountainside I climbed over boulders the size of small cars, and then I entered the bush.

By now it was almost completely dark and all I could do was keep descending towards the river. It was a long way. Far, far longer than I had thought from above.

When I reached the river it was pitch black and I trod through marsh and reeds to get to the water for a drink. Then I stamped about amongst the reeds wondering what I should do.

It was perishingly cold and there was ice at the edge of the river. I knew I was dehydrated so I drank quite a lot, but the cold water chilled me more.

At last I remembered the red nylon garment in my rucksack and I pulled it out.

It had a zip on each side, so, shivering all the time, I did up the zips, and what emerged was a pair of red nylon shorts with a sort of huge upper part to go right up my chest reaching underneath my armpits almost to my neck.

I put on this extraordinary garment and pondered on the oddities of New Zealanders. "Who on earth would invent such an absurd pair of shorts, for god's sake!?" I thought.

Later, much later, I realised what I had done; I had joined up the zips in the wrong way. Had I done it properly I would have had a pair of red, nylon long overtrousers – up to my waist, with a zip down the side of each leg!

But in the dark and the cold, and shivering so intensely it had not entered my head to try the zips the other way.

Thus clad in red nylon shorts that went up to my chest I shivered and stamped and cogitated all night long, trying to decide on a plan for the morrow.

The hours passed and I shivered continuously.

It was an hour or two before dawn that I made the decision to climb back up the way I had descended and try to find my way up the ridge and down to the rock wall, then to descend it alone and with no rope.

But as soon as I began climbing I realised how cold, weak and dehydrated I was.

I made slow progress uphill in the dense bush where I could see only several feet in any direction because of the trees.

The sun rose, and I clawed my way on up.

The morning was advancing and I still had not emerged above the bush. At this rate, I thought, I could be all day just climbing up to the ridge – then the thought occurred to me that it might be a regular phenomenon for the clouds to gather thickly on the mountain in the afternoon, and I began to think that if that were to be the case I could end up in exactly the same situation, in dense cloud, as I had been twenty-four hours previously.

So I sat down in the bush, clinging to roots, and tried to devise another plan.

It was at that moment that the earthquake struck.

Then I recalled the glimmer of light I had seen in the distance from my view point high above the bush as I had descended below the cloud the previous day. Could it be Lake Rotoroa?

I tried to visualise the map so briefly glimpsed two days before.

I think there had been one or maybe two lakes on the map, and both had been to the North of Mt Hopeless.

Yes, I should head North and hope to reach the lake.

So I descended through the bush once again and, once again, drank at the river's edge.

At least it was relatively flat by the river, although its banks were thick with bush.

I pushed North, following the river, finding my way first on one bank then on the other, depending on the thickness of the bush on each side. Each crossing was thigh or waist deep, and I crossed many times.

I was able to drink, and that was important, for the day was very hot.

Soon I took off my bizarre nylon shorts and, still puzzled by their design, I put them in my pack.

After many hours I felt I was making some progress.

I had to keep constantly reminding myself that in the southern hemisphere the sun does not cross the southern part of the sky, but to the North. This fact is a little disconcerting to someone from England, because instinct and habit told me that shadows point northwards in the middle of the day....but I had to keep my head and not make silly mistakes.

At one point the bush in which I was struggling got steeper and steeper and I could hear the roar of a waterfall. Then in front of me emerged a place where the river, normally fifty metres wide, had funnelled down to a three metre gap and it was cascading down into a pool some 100 feet below.

Across this waterfall I could see the other side where the bush was less dense. Should I attempt to jump across?

It looked just possible to jump.

I scrutinised the far bank and saw that a large boulder provided a fairly flat surface. The distance between me and the boulder was about nine feet, and the boulder was a few feet below my level.

If I jumped very hard across the waterfall I could land on the boulder, I thought.

Then I saw how the surface of the boulder was green with moss, probably damp from the spray of the waterfall, and I looked down at the rocky pool a hundred feet below and reconsidered!

It would have been too dangerous to jump across, I decided, so I had to retrace my steps back up the steep bush and cross the river maybe a mile or two back.

It all took a long time – which was why I had so seriously considered making the jump!

Having crossed the river I continued making my way north. After half an hour the trees became thinner and after a couple of miles my nostrils were assailed by a smell. At first I couldn't identify it, then it struck me – bacon frying! And a half mile further on there was a plume of blue smoke rising from the river bank.

Civilisation!

I approached the small group of backpackers who were surprised to see me. They gave me a bacon sandwich which I gladly accepted but I found it hard to swallow, so dry was my mouth.

The hikers told me where I was, some distance South of Lake Rotoroa. If I headed a couple of hundred yards through the bush to the West, away from the river, I would come across a marked trail, they said, and the going would be easier by far on the trail rather than struggling through the bush. They sent me on my way with words of advice and soon I found the trail. I had been close to it, but had been unaware of it.

I followed the marked trail North with a lighter heart now that I had a clear idea of the situation.

I reached the lake in the late afternoon, and there indeed, as the hikers had told me, were some families fishing from boats.

I found a log cabin on the lake shore and went inside and made tea for myself on the stove. I drank several cups.

An hour or so later a figure entered the hut and I asked the man if he would give me a lift up the lake in his boat, and he readily agreed.

At the top end of the lake I thanked him as I got out of his boat, and I walked up to the Park Ranger's hut and explained who I was and what had happened.

I asked the ranger if he had news of Tom and John, but he had not.

I told him the story of the climb and the wind howling and the boulders (or bodies?) falling and how I had had to come down alone. He said he would launch a search.

Nightfall found me hitching a lift back to Blenheim….no easy matter when the flow of traffic averaged about one car every two hours – and the first car did not stop!

Later I learned what had become of Tom and John. They had climbed up through thickening cloud and taken longer than they had expected. Eventually they had turned back below the summit in worsening weather and had reached the meeting point at my notch on the ridge considerably later than they had intended.

Not finding me, they had descended to the hut and there, still unable to find me, they had searched the area in darkness for a while before going into the hut to sleep.

Next morning they had searched again for me, especially around the foot of the rock face, and then eventually they had given up and walked out the way they had come, arriving at the Park Ranger's hut that evening only a couple of hours after I had passed through.

Thus ended a weekend which, for me at least, was named rather aptly, like the mountain, Hopeless!

A Good Night Out.

"There's an igloo meet next weekend on the summit of Aonach Mhor," said Dave.

It was early March 1993 and I had accompanied Dave Ashworth on some of his igloo meets in previous years.

Ben Nevis and Brairiach come to mind.

Each Winter the Rucksack Club, of which Dave is a longtime member, hold a meet on the summit of a 3,000ft Scottish peak - a different one each year - and each member has to reach the summit and build an igloo and sleep the night in it.

The night out on Ben Nevis had been magic. Dave and I had reached the summit by Gardyloo Gully and when night fell the moon looked down on a dozen igloos. When the occupants lit candles inside, each igloo glowed in the dark like a lightbulb. That night the weather had been clear and freezing and still and we were all cosy in our sleeping bags. Some people had built interconnecting tunnels so that a whisky bottle could the more easily be passed around the group.

And then on Brairiach it had been a long steep haul up from Loch Morlich, through the "Charlemagne Gap", and over the top of the Lairig Ghru and on to the Brairiach summit plateau....all this after a 5 a.m. start and a long drive North from Windermere.

The cutting of the snow blocks, and the laying of them round and round, higher and leaning inwards, had been executed more quickly because we had become more adept, and also because of the lateness of the hour. But the views down the corries the next morning, as the sun rose, looking over a blanket of cloud lying deep in the valleys, had been memorable.

So when Dave asked me to join him for a similar trip to Aonach Mhor I readily agreed.

I packed my rucksack with sleeping bag, foam mat for insulation, bivvy bag, duvet jacket, big gloves, boots, gaiters, balaclava and also paraffin stove, pan and some food. To cut the snow blocks I carried a handsaw of the woodwork variety, and also a snow shovel, useful for lifting blocks up from the ground.

Eamon, a retired teacher from Windermere, had agreed to join us, and so it was the three of us who jumped into a car and drove up North from Windermere that Saturday morning. A little over four hours to Glencoe, then another one and a half hours up to the Aonach Mhor car park just North of Fort William, and we unloaded our stuff and bought tickets for the cable car up to the ski slopes.

The weather looked bad.

As we ascended the mountain the wind buffeted our cablecar and we became aware of large numbers of people coming down on the lifts and few indeed going up.

On arriving at the lift station we were told by the ski patrol that the mountain was being "closed down" to skiers because of high winds. The man in charge ordered us to turn around and go down.

"But we're not skiers," we said, "We're meeting a group on the summit of Aonach Mhor to build igloos." His reply was carried away on the wind but we were obviously in a distinct minority with everyone except us going down.

We could see the chairs on the chairlifts being swung violently from side to side in the powerful gusts of wind. The surface of the snow was obscured by a layer of spindrift driven at high speed by the wind.

The cables on the T-bar lifts were stretched out between their pylons as the wind plucked sideways at them.

It never entered our heads to turn around.

We shouldered our packs and set off up the mountain following the lifts towards the summit of Aonach Mhor.

Halfway up we came across the last skier being blown at speed across the mountainside as he tried to descend to the lift station escorted by a couple of ski patrollers who shouted incoherently at us before they were swallowed up in the spindrift.

Up we struggled until we reached the top of the uppermost line of pylons.

By now the wind was so strong that it was impossible to talk to each other even when shouting with one's mouth right up against the other's ear.

There was a little wooden hut visible thirty yards away and we made for that. It was the lift attendant's hut and in its shelter we were just able to communicate with each other, shouting mouth to ear.

A short discussion ensued.

The hour was getting late and the top was still a few hundred yards away, but we were sure that we would meet the other Rucksack Club igloo-builders there, so we decided to press on and meet up with them, and have a go at building our igloo, and if after a decent try we were unsuccessful, then we would head back down. We thought we'd give ourselves forty-five minutes to see how we got on.

Dave and I were confident that with our saws and shovel we could get the structure built quite quickly and from previous experience we knew we would be well sheltered once inside.

So we advanced.

On the summit words were impossible. They were torn from one's throat and hurled into the screaming force that gripped us.

There was no sign of anybody else on the summit, and, using gestures, Dave suggested that I walk on further into the vortex to see if perhaps there might be a cluster of igloos a bit further on.

But I, aware as I was of the proximity of cliffs in that region, and unable to see because the icy particles were slamming into my eyes at colossal speed carried on the wind, took out a rope and tied on, and advanced cautiously only when I knew Dave was belaying me. With head down and turned away from the wind and leaning forwards almost to forty-five degrees I pushed ahead for a hundred yards or so, but there was no sign of anyone.

And so we started cutting snow blocks - or should I say ice blocks, for there was precious little real snow on the summit, just a hard layer of ice and a thin pack of snow with boulders protruding.

We cut with our saws – a process made difficult by the fact that the wind seized the saw blade and tried to wrench it from our grasp. When the saw blade was in the air it was as if an invisible hand was trying to tear it away.

The gusts were so powerful that we could not put down our

packs; they would have been blown away. So we worked as quickly as we could, Eamon and I cutting blocks and handing them to Dave who started building a circular structure.

We were surprised to find that although there was so little real snow the ice blocks which we cut seemed to remain intact, and although they were thin they were beginning to form the wall of an igloo.

We built upwards and became engrossed in our task so that three quarters of an hour passed without us noticing, and already the igloo was more than half built.

We felt that we could succeed in completing it and worked harder and harder. The final roof block was lifted into place as darkness closed in around us.

Still there was no let-up in the gale.

I went inside the igloo and began to assemble the stove for cooking.

Inside one could take off one's pack, but, although the general force of the wind was less inside than out, the structure of the wall contained hundreds of tiny holes where each block abutted against its neighbour, and through these holes the air was accelerated as it entered the igloo and left by the door.

So I sat inside with a hundred icy jetstreams blasting at me as I tried to ignite the stove, and before long spindrift had covered me, my sack, and the stove.

We had to seal the holes.

But the spindrift was so fine and icy that one could not use it as one normally would use snow when igloo building, packing it into holes and crevices to seal them. Normally one can round off the outer and inner surfaces using gloved hands and a saw, and one can seal all the holes so that the building is cosy and draught proof inside.

Indeed one of the most curious things about an igloo is how very silent it is inside. Someone can be standing outside shouting but you cannot hear him, unless of course he pokes his head into the entrance!

And so we set to, cutting yet more icy blocks, and this time laying them like a second layer all around the first, trying to place the blocks in such a way as to overlap the holes in the first layer. It was hard work, and it was thanks to Dave's tenacity that we got as much done as we did.

Finally, with the roar of the wind blasting stronger than ever, we crawled in through the opening and laid out our sleeping bags and got into them fully clothed except for boots.

The paraffin stove was choked with snow; it would not ignite.

But Dave, resourceful as ever, had brought with him not only storm matches (waterproof and to a certain extent windproof) but also an Epigas stove, and with this lit we were able to cheer up the inside of our home, melt some ice and heat it for a drink, and also eventually to get the paraffin stove lit and heat something to eat

At this point I feel I should make some remarks about food.

Dave and I had ventured into the hills on many occasions and had developed somewhat of a banter between us when it came to food.

He, for example, would extract from his sack tasty meals of chicken and rice, or of lamb and vegetables, often prepared by Messrs Marks and Spencer. He would cook them in a lightweight pan and smack his lips to show how delicious they were.

I on the other hand had a tendency to assume the image of a caveman; I brought a cast iron pan and some lentils and cabbage or some such, and sometimes I would pull out a packet of dehydrated grot from years gone by going by the name of "Stew - Beef Flavour (Best Before 1976) - Manufactured From Soya Protein."

This packet was brandished around in various locations over a number of years, and the "Best Before" date receded further and further into the past as we habitually declined to open it, he with expletives, and me with a comment such as, "Oh well then. We'll save it for when we really need it!"

I rather think the offending packet made its appearance for the last time that night; perhaps that night was the night we really did need it.

Anyhow the meal we had was a mixture of whatever we all produced from our packs and was well mixed up with spindrift. We swallowed it down and tried to make ourselves as comfortable as we could using head torches to see in the dark.

The wind continued as strong as ever and its roar was, if anything, intensified inside the igloo because the icy jets of air screeched like demons as each jet tore through our double layer of ice, finding its way through all the holes.

The only comparison I can think of is that it was like lying down in a deep freezer in a railway tunnel with express trains roaring through all night long incessantly.

The night was spent huddled together in the pitch dark with spindrift finding its way inexorably into our sleeping bags and down our necks – and the roar of the wind still so deafening as to make conversation virtually impossible.

It was not a very comfortable night, and I for one slept hardly at all.

Dave, who has an immense capacity for sleeping soundly in all circumstances, mingled his snores with the howling of the wind.

Eamon was silent. We were each wrapped in our own world with our own thoughts.

Mine were mostly to do with getting down in the morning!

When a hint of light was discernible after the long night of intense cold and incessant noise, I put on my head torch and was aghast to see that our bodies were covered with about two feet of snow.

We were all three buried underneath the spindrift which had blown in through all the tiny holes in the wall of our igloo!

I put on my boots which I had kept inside my sleeping bag, and stirred the other two.

Dave quickly got himself organised, emerging from underneath his thick blanket of snow.

Eamon, however, had not kept his boots safe inside his sleeping bag.

His boots were lost somewhere underneath all the spindrift and he was seriously cold.

Dave found the lost boots and helped Eamon on with them and we quickly packed our gear, and crawled out through the tunnel exit of the igloo.

We got to our feet and started to head downhill.

I do not know what time it was, perhaps about 6 a.m., but the velocity of the wind was little different from what it had been all night.

As we started down the ski slopes my saw, which had been lashed to one of our rucksacks, rocketed up into the air and shot off downwind like an arrow, never to be seen again.

We walked as fast as we could, Eamon struggling more with the cold than Dave or me, and we kept going down, down until we eventually reached the upper lift station.

Not a soul was around.

The station was shut and locked.

After a brief pause at the station we carried on down the steep mountainside for the few miles it took till we reached the car park at the bottom where I arrived at about 8.30 a.m. followed several minutes later by Dave who had stuck close by Eamon.

At the car park, which was a few thousand feet lower than the summit, things were calmer, less cold, less serious, and we were able to reflect on our night of survival.

I think we were all somewhat stunned by what we had been through and how serious the conditions had been - worse by far than any that Dave or I had ever experienced in Scotland.

We drove to the supermarket in Fort William where there is a cafeteria and we ordered a large breakfast each.

I seem to recall ordering a second one too - it's not often that I eat two full English breakfasts in a row!

We took stock of our situation and were able to laugh and chat about it all, but the reality had been touch and go, and we must have been close to suffering from exposure in a very dangerous situation.

Later we learned that none of the other Rucksack clubbers had gone up the hill; all of them had thought the weather forecast too bad.

Some had ventured up towards the summit of Aonach Mhor earlier in the day before, only to turn around when they felt the force of the wind.

Of course, had we known all this, it is probable that we too would, like them, have spent the evening in the pub in the valley, but it was partly our certainty that we would meet friends on the summit that had kept us going.

Some time later I had occasion, out of curiosity, to phone the meteorological station at Fort William and ask them if they had any data on weather conditions for Saturday March 7th 1993. “Yes, we do,” they told me. “There were big gales then. The wind speeds were recorded as averaging 75 m.p.h. at our highest station which is a thousand feet below Aonach Mhor summit, and gusts of over 100 m.p.h. were recorded. On the summit we have no station, but there would have been considerably higher speeds on the summit. Why do you want to know?”

So I explained.

The Sherpa's Finger.

It was 1989 and I joined a group of several climbers from the Oldham Mountaineering Club to do a trek and a climb in Nepal.

A trekking peak called Chulu East, which lies to the North of the Annapurna massif, had been chosen as our objective.

Trekking peaks are so-called because they are ostensibly capable of being climbed by trekkers and they do not require a mountaineering permit, but one should beware of underrating their difficulties because every year there are deaths on the trekking peaks of Nepal and one must be experienced and equipped to tackle them.

We assembled at Heathrow airport and surveyed our pile of gear. There were ropes, crampons, ice-axes, light weight high altitude tents, snow stakes, karabiners, as well as rucksacks of personal gear.

The flight to Katmandu was via Bangladesh where flies hovered over sticky brown food available at the airport canteen.

Once arrived in Katmandu, Nepal, we were met by Ang Zangbu of Highland Sherpa, the trekking organisation, and taken to our hotel in town. We handed over all our gear for distribution to the team of porters who would be accompanying us, and enjoyed a day's relaxation before our bus journey to Ghurka, from where we would set out on our trek anti-clockwise round the Annapurna range of mountains.

Next day after a ride of several hours, the dusty, bumpy bus deposited us in the late afternoon and we filed out across the lowland rice fields for a trek that would last three weeks.

Each night camp was set up at a preordained site, dictated, by and large, by the porters, whose daily distance could not be expected to exceed several hours of walking. One did not measure distance in miles, but rather in hours or days, because the terrain was steep for the most part, either up or down, and stops were frequent.

We gained height slowly but surely as we worked our way day by day up the Marsyangdi Kola valley, passing through little villages where one could stop and have a cup of hot tea, a bowl of rice and lentils, or some of the delicious little green oranges which were for sale.

Each village is pleased to see trekkers who spend a little money as they pass by, and tourism (in the form of trekking) is such a vital part of Nepal's economy that the remote villages generally ensure that they are well stocked with Fanta and Star beer all of which have to be carried in on the backs of porters to reach their various destinations often many days walking up into the hills - so that one can almost tell what the altitude is by the price of the beer!

The walk was a most delightful experience and we were a friendly group.

Our sirdar (he is the one in charge of all the porters) was called Nawang. He was a man of mature years and considerable experience and he had the uncanny ability to keep his plimsoles unblemished and pristine white throughout the entire expedition. How he managed to keep them so clean I do not know, because the track was often muddy.

I recall how Rod Campbell and I would discuss this achievement and we would try to find out Nawang's secret....but we never did.

We would watch him on the muddy sections where everybody ended up with filthy boots – that is everybody except Nawang!

We would spy on him in the camp to see if he had spare pairs of plimsoles or tins of cleaning fluid.....but he appeared to have only one pair – and the ability to float over the surface of puddles!

I rather think that Nawang regarded us all as amateurs whilst he was the professional!

Sometimes during meals in the evenings he would hint at major Himalayan peaks that he had scaled, of serious climbs that he had led, and of famous mountaineers whom he knew or with whom he had associated.

Obviously our little trip was an easy vacation for him.

Anyhow, his clean white plimsoles were the daily trademark of this man and testimony to a life of experience!

Time was relatively short, however, and if we were to succeed in our intended climb as well as the circular trek we needed to keep going.

After ten days we entered the flatter Manang valley and, looking Westwards along it, we could see Pisang Peak to the North of the valley, and beyond that, still out of sight, was Chulu.

As we passed along the floor of the valley we at last came to the village of Ongre from which we gained a spectacular view of the Annapurna peaks soaring high into the sky to the South, and up a side valley to the North of Ongre we could see the Chulus.

There was supposed to be a Chulu East, and a Chulu West, and a Chulu Far East, but the various maps and descriptions we had were at odds with each other and it was uncertain which was which.

We spent a night in Ongre, where the locals sang Nepalese songs and we retaliated with raucous renderings of the Hokey Cokey and Ilkla Moor Baht 'At, and next day we headed up the side valley towards the Chulus, some of us with headaches, even though the altitude was not yet great!

It was a steep pull of several hours and we were all feeling the effects of altitude by the time we made camp beside a little mountain river.

This was to be our base camp.

At night it was noticeably much colder than it had been on the valley floor in Ongre about three thousand feet below us.

We found it amazing that the porters could survive as they did without sleeping bags.

They huddled together, covering themselves with a blanket each, smoking fiercely, and emerged in the morning none the worse.

The "dawn chorus" was an event which occurred daily, and it was something that one got used to when trekking, for the still morning air would be rent with the sound of the porters coughing and hawking up great gobbets of phlegm from their chests. This would go on for several minutes.

In villages, where hens scratched around in the dirt on the trails, one would often come across a hen greedily pecking at a rich yellow or green gob of phlegm recently expectorated from a passing porter.

When eating eggs we would often amuse ourselves with such observations.

But now we had left the valley and the view from base camp was truly spectacular. We were at an altitude of about 10,000 ft, and were situated some 3,000 ft above the valley floor. The Annapurna range was spread in front of our eyes.

Higher up behind us a waterfall fell a hundred metres through space over a cliff, and where it landed there was a massive cone of ice.

We had to find a way up to the right of this waterfall and then up into the valley above it.

The ascent was steep and the altitude was taking its toll on various members of the team who wisely decided to rest at base camp. But six of us felt able to continue and this we did, arriving at a point high above the waterfall to make a second camp at 13,000 ft.

Here there were only boulders and ice and in the thin air we moved slowly.

From here we could clearly discern Chulu East as it rose into the sky, all snowy white, to the Northwest.

To its right, farther East, was a second big mountain and the name of this was, we thought, Chulu Far East - but there was an uncertainty as to which was which, and on some maps it appeared named as Chulu West, even though it was farther East.

Climbing the wrong mountain seemed to be a distinct possibility!

The next day, as Tony, Rod, Alan, Richard, Dave and myself

walked very slowly up to our high camp at about 15,000 ft at the foot of both mountains, we met a Spanish party coming down.

They had climbed the peak to the right.

They were able to tell us about the route they had climbed, and we also asked them about Chulu East (which was to the West!) and they explained that it was higher and more difficult and a longer route than the one they had climbed, and would probably require two or three days to reach the summit and get back down.

The problem apparently was that the base of the big Northeast ridge on Chulu East (and this ridge seemed to be the way up to the summit) could only be reached by crossing over a rocky col, and then dropping down a pitch in order to get onto a high glacier which fell away at a steep angle for a couple of hundred feet eventually to abut against the ridge which led up the mountain.

So one first had to climb a short distance above camp to get up to the col, then cross it to the other side, and climb down onto the glacier, then descend the glacier, dropping a few hundred feet to the foot of the ridge, then climb the long ridge up to the summit.

Very probably a bivouac would be required on the ridge halfway up to the summit.

Then on the descent all these difficulties would have to be reversed, but no doubt in a tired state and perhaps dehydrated.

A bivouac would necessitate carrying much gear and a stove and food, and consequently movement would be slower at such altitude.

In all probability this route would require a minimum of three days.

We had too little time considering the fact that we had taken a couple of days longer than we had expected to reach the mountain, and also the fact that we had still a long trek and a steep high pass to cross to complete the circuit of the Annapurnas and reach Pokhara before getting a bus back to Katmandu and then to fly home on a fixed date.

All this posed somewhat of a logistical problem.

The Spanish party's sherpa, however, who spoke very little English, managed to communicate with us using sign language and a scanty vocabulary, and he said that he had heard that a party of Japanese had found a one-day route up Chulu East by means of a gully leading from a high snow basin up onto the higher reaches of the summit ridge.

This high snow basin was apparently not too far above the campsite and was on this side of the mountain, so the route he was suggesting would avoid us dropping down the steep glacier, and it would miss out most of the Northeast ridge.

He thought it could be done in a day.

As he spoke he pointed at the mountain and tried to explain where the gully in question was.

We huddled round the sherpa trying hard to understand the information he had to give us.

We gathered that it might indeed be possible to go up and down Chulu East in one day via this gully rather than the anticipated three days by the other route on its Northeast ridge.

I squinted carefully along his finger as he pointed up in the direction of the high snow basin and the gully above it.

Both these were out of sight from where we were standing.

Then the Spanish party bid us goodbye and dropped quickly down the mountain.

At high camp we went through our gear and plans.

Rod Campbell and Tony were intending to tackle Chulu Far East via the route recently climbed by the Spanish party we had met.

Alan, Dave and I decided to have a try at Chulu East and its snow gully.

It would be a long hard day ahead of us.

We went early to the tent and rose at midnight.

After a brew of tea we set off across the moraine by the light of our headtorches. After a few hundred metres we put on crampons and picked our way up steeper ground on ice and rock till we found ourselves on a subsidiary ridge. We made our way up and over this in the pitch dark and we found ourselves on an obvious way which led us up over a rising snowfield to a large snow basin in the heart of the mountain.

It was still dark at 5 a.m. when we reached the far side of the snow basin and sat down for a rest at the base of a wall up which some snow gullies slanted - but it was hard to see in the dark, so we waited for dawn.

But waiting made us so cold that it was not long before we decided we had to keep moving. We had been on the go nearly six hours and had a very long way still to climb. We must not delay. So we roped up and started to climb the steep snow and ice directly above us.

Was this the gully indicated by the sherpa's pointed finger?

We would find out.

We tackled the ascent pitch by pitch as the sun came and brought warmth.

The gully was not too hard, but we did not know how long it was nor what surprises it might contain for us.

We could see a rope-length above us, but no more.

Slowly but surely we gained height, but it was getting late in the morning when we emerged at the top of the gully and found ourselves high on the main ridge.

We were evidently well up the mountain and with the summit visible above us.

Below us the Northeast ridge dropped steeply down.

The gully had proved to be about 1,000 ft long and it was indeed a shortcut to the upper part of the mountain.

Distance was difficult to gauge, and time even more so, but I reckoned on another hour to the summit with perhaps six or seven hundred feet of vertical ascent.

However the way to the summit did look to be clear and did not appear to contain much in the way of difficulties from that point on.

We sat for several minutes, dozy in the heat of the sun, and stared out over the rocky peaks of Tibet which lay to the North side of Chulu. They looked barren and uninviting.

I tried to drink from my water bottle, but its contents were frozen solid - as they had been all day.

Dave was exhausted with the altitude and Alan and I prevailed upon him to stay where he was and ascend no further.

He was somewhat reluctant to do this but his pace was too slow by now, and his slowness was proving to be a danger to all three of us.

If we did not reach the summit and begin the descent by 1 p.m. we risked being benighted.

Dave (and I must say at this point, this is an entirely different Dave from the Dave Ashworth of the igloo story) was not actually a member of our expedition but he had been walking around the Annapurnas in the same direction as us and had been on his own.

He was carrying all his own gear and had chanced upon us in a village several days back and had joined up with us: in fact he and Alan were acquainted with each other having met previously in other foreign parts - so he had fallen in with us for the climb.

So it was Alan and I who continued slowly up to the summit.

Every step required heavy breathing and, as is so often the case, each time we thought the summit was reached we saw yet higher ground above us.

However we eventually reached the top where we took a few photos and surveyed the scene before turning around for the descent.

From where we stood on the summit we could look over onto the peaks of Chulu Far East and Chulu West.

We could see how advanced was the day, and also how clouds were gathering in the valleys far below us. The weather looked as if it might worsen.

We were able to take in our surroundings rather than focussing on the next few steps uphill, as we had been for several hours.

One loses track of time so easily on such an ascent, particularly if experiencing fatigue and dehydration, and we needed to make haste yet remain careful.

It was already just past midday and we had the entire descent to make.

What had taken us nearly two hours to climb, took maybe half an hour or less to descend, and we were soon back at the top of the gully with Dave.

We roped up and began to descend the gully.

Dave needed much encouragement, I recall, and we had to make a number of abseils as well as an abseil down a fairly steep ice pitch.

Descending snow and ice is always far harder than climbing it, and we moved slowly and carefully.

It was about half past three in the afternoon when we arrived at the snow basin at the foot of the gully. We made our way separately back to the camp.

I reached camp at about five o'clock having been on the go for almost seventeen hours, and still my water flask was frozen!

Night was approaching.

I felt very tired and dehydrated but revived after several cups of tea and noodle soup.

In my pocket was a bar of chocolate at which I had from time to time gnawed, but it had remained more or less intact, so dry was my mouth.

The other two reached camp an hour or so later, and the porters who had come with us to high camp were kept busy making tea and noodle soup for us for a long time.

The next day we heard that Rod and Tony had been successful too in their climb.

We spent the morning exchanging experiences and then we all packed up and headed downhill.

It was amazing how easy it was to descend. What had taken so many days to climb took scarcely a morning to come down, and it was not long before we passed the waterfall and reached base camp.

That night at base camp we had a big celebration and Jangbo, the cook, made us a special cake. Rod entertained everyone with Django Reinhardt impressions, which called for a remarkable talent particularly with a mouth full of special cake, and considering the altitude, and the absence of a guitar.

His performance was met with polite applause all round.

Next day we reached the valley floor and continued our walk via the town of Manang and then, two days later, we came to the foot of the Thorong La pass.

This pass climbs to a height of over 17,000 ft and is flanked by two gigantic snow peaks at its highest point.

There were many other trekkers trying to get over the pass, and some failed to do so because of the altitude and breathlessness. Indeed there had been two young women we had met in the village of Manang who had said that they had made repeated efforts to cross the pass heading West but had failed, and they had been sitting in Manang contemplating a return journey back along the way they had walked over the previous fortnight.

Some of the trekkers, who were evidently struggling up the Thorong La approaching the high point of the pass, were in need of assistance from their sherpas and porters, and one or two, I noted, had to be carried over the pass and down the first thousand foot of the descent.

I dropped down over the pass to reach the village of Muktinath several thousand feet below.

Next day the trail continued its slow descent via Jomosom, Morpha and Kalo Pani, and I wandered on till I found a place for the night in a tiny house where I was kindly put up by a man and his wife at Koketaki.

This was a most delightful walk for it was all downhill and with a small pack and the warm sunshine it felt as if I had wings on my feet.

At Tatopani, several hours further down the Kali Gandaki valley, there were hot springs and good food. It was truly blissful to relax in the warm water and stare up at the huge peaks.

The remainder of the trek was a wonderful succession of pretty little hospitable villages, excellent food served by attractive Nepalese girls, and exhilarating views of mountains all around.

The days flowed past with a rhythm of their own such as one only finds on long walks, accompanied by changing scenery and simple but excellent food purchased in the villages en route.

The track climbed up to the little village of Ghorapani where I spent my last night on the trail. Behind the village is a hill from the top of which are the most magnificent views of Annapurna South and Dhaulagiri. I watched the sun set from the hill top and returned to the village, but decided to rise early to see the next day dawn.

I got out of bed after a few hours sleep and climbed the hill, for a second time, but this time in the dark, only to discover that the dawn was taking a little longer to arrive than I had calculated.

Standing around in the dark was getting too cold for me so I walked about a bit and when I came back to the hill top I saw a Japanese man kneeling on the ground as the first rays of the sun came over Annapurna.

He was intent on performing some sort of ceremony and appeared to be wrapping a length of material around his head.

It was a white bandana with Japanese writing on it.

His actions were rather reminiscent of pictures of Kamikaze pilots that I had seen on films doing that sort of thing.

He fumbled in a bag beside him on the ground and I feared he was going to commit Hari Kiri or whatever it is called and that he was about to pull a knife from his bag.

I was on the point of going over to him and tapping him on the shoulder and saying, "Hold on, old chap! Let's not be too hasty!" or something like that, when he saw me and grinned broadly and showed me his Nikon camera with a formidable array of accessory lenses in the bag.

I returned to the village of Ghorapani after sunrise and had a bite to eat before setting off on the long, last day's walk on the trail to Pokhara, which I reached in the early evening.

Next day a bus carried me back to Katmandu and down to earth.

Of Rocks And Rivers.

Sometimes everything just falls into place.

It happened so one week in July in 1983.

I had been introduced to Alan Hopper by Jonty Ward.

Jonty was at that time building a windmill near the Fylde coast (just one of those things you would expect Jonty to do!), and Alan was doing the joinery for him.

And so it was that Alan and I, both keen on rock climbing, found ourselves heading up to Scotland together.

And, what's more, it was a heatwave!

My memories of that week are all good ones - except for one; so I shall start with that.

The upper reaches of the River Etive, at the top of Glencoe, cascade over waterfalls into deep pools where the swimming is wonderful. There are several such pools and it was into one of these that I dived at the end of the day we had spent climbing on the Etive Slabs.

The water was deep and dark and cool and you cannot have any better experience than a swim in such a pool after getting hot and sweaty on a walk or a climb.

I swam across the pool and clambered up the rocks on the other side and looked back to see what Alan was doing. I had told him the best swimming pools imaginable were here in Glen Etive, and he had said "Why aye, man!" an expression which Geordies often tend to use, so I had thought he was pleased at the prospect.

Unfortunately, as I looked around I could not see Alan, who had definitely been standing on the rock at the edge of the pool only a few moments before, and it was after several seconds that I spotted a human arm sticking up out of the river and sort of waving at me.

At first I wondered what the hell he was doing just submerging himself and waving with one hand, but then I realised that the gesture was intended to indicate distress!

I am not a fast swimmer, but I did my best to emulate Tarzan pursued by a shark as I raced back to the other side again and helped Alan, who was still submerged but struggling to extricate himself.

Minutes later, when we had both recovered our breath I asked him "What happened?" and he replied saying that he had just plunged into the pool having quite forgotten that he could not swim! Then, finding himself in water about twelve foot deep, and, seeing as how he was nowhere near twelve foot tall, his feet had been unable to touch the bottom, he had begun to experience the sensation of drowning and, wisely, had raised his hand to attract my attention.

Well, all's well that ends well, and after a bit of spluttering and coughing up quantities of the River Etive Alan showed no untoward effects.

He sensibly decided that in future it might be more propitious to test the depth of water in a pool before plunging in, and the remainder of that week gave plenty of opportunity for him to do so.

Earlier that day we had climbed two routes on the Etive Slabs, which are on the North Eastern flanks of Buchaille Etive Mhor, Glencoe. The first was Spartan Slabs which starts just left of the Coffin Stone and which ascends over 600 ft of grooves, slabs, cracks and bulges. On such a dry day the friction was superb and the climbing was exhilarating.

Next we made for Hammer, which is at the left end of the crag, and which is a shorter but harder route. Near the start there is a nervously holdless scoop up which one must step boldly in order to reach a large vertical corner. I can recall hesitating for a long time and making several tentative but feeble attempts before plucking up the courage to step more positively up the scoop.

Alan tackled the steep corner and then the big traverse right underneath the roof and up the overlap to make the exit at the top.

After camping the night we spent the next day on the steep Rannoch Wall of the Buchaille where we climbed Agag's Groove with its excellent holds and impressive exposure, then January Jigsaw.

The sun kept on shining and conditions were perfect.

The following day we set off for Ben Nevis and walked up the Allt a Mhuillin track until we arrived at the base of the Orion Face.

Scrambling up the scree we came to the foot of Zero Gully and roped up in the cool shade of the cliffs. Despite the heatwave there was still plenty of snow forming a cone at the base of Zero Gully. Across this we trod to reach the first pitch of The Long Climb which works its way for 1,430 ft up the Orion Face of Ben Nevis and is regarded as the greatest route put up by J. H. B. Bell in 1940.

The climb is full of interest and easy pitches are intermingled with steeper, harder ones until we emerged several hours later right on the summit of the Ben. It had been a classic climb and the end of the day brought a sense of satisfaction in having completed it.

We headed north once more, this time bound for the Loch Laggan road where we left the car near Moy Lodge and walked South to Binnein Shuas.

The day was hot as ever, not a cloud in the sky.

Above us was "the best route in the country", some say - Ardverikie Wall.

We put on harnesses and roped up, leaving our sacks at the foot of the climb.

There followed one of the most enjoyable climbing experiences for me, where the holds were all there - but only just, and protection was also there - but in some places only just.

The cliff rose steeply up from the undergrowth at the base of the crag, and the loch below sparkled invitingly.

The heat bounced off the rock.

Each pitch was full of interest and challenge and the two of us worked our way upwards with immense satisfaction.

On returning to our packs we felt unable to resist the temptation to plunge into the loch for a swim - at least for me a swim, and for Alan whatever you call it when you can't swim but just have a great time splashing around in the water.

I have returned to that climb a few times in later years, and always enjoyed it, but never as much as on that first visit.

Our travels took us then farther North past the Seven Sisters of Kintail and into Wester Ross.

We reached the little village of Lochcarron in the evening and had something to eat. Then we drove on a few miles in the direction of Applecross until the road goes over a little bridge under which the Russel Burn flows downhill from Loch Coire Nan Arr and into the sea at Loch Kishorn.

In front of us we could see the road winding steeply up to the Pass of the Cattle.

It was ten o'clock in the evening and we were tired and hot .

We pulled the car over and made our way down to the river's edge.

We brewed some tea, talked of this and that, and spread out our sleeping bags on a flat boulder.

In the North of Scotland it does not get properly dark in the middle of a Summer's night; and so we lay down as the light began to fade and were soon asleep. Too hot to get inside our sleeping bags, we just lay on top of them. I remember the midges being somewhat of a nuisance, but we slept soundly despite them.

In the morning it was the heat, once again, which awoke us.

Our destination that day was Sgurr a Chaorachain, also called The Cioch, which is a big red sandstone buttress located a couple of miles up the valley to our North West.

We shouldered our rucksacks and set off uphill.

Soon we crossed a little mountain stream cascading downhill in a series of waterfalls, and above it and beyond we could see The

Cioch.

The steep buttress looked imposing, but the guidebook said that on it was a route called The Cioch Nose, described as "The Diff to end all Diffs." So said Chris Bonnington who climbed it first in 1960 with Tom Patey.

Its reputation was that, although it was steep and looked hard from below, it had a veritable plethora of huge jug holds which came to hand just when you needed them.

With our expectations high we approached the cliff.

We were not disappointed.

Pitch followed pitch as the sun beat down on us from a clear blue sky.

Alan and I revelled in the enjoyment of climbing such a magnificent route in such isolation.

Not a soul was to be seen.

It was like magic the way each upward movement, each hand reaching high and groping the hot rock, was met with exactly what was needed - a large handhold.

There are those who despise relatively easy climbs, preferring to lodge the tip of one finger in a tiny crevice and to pull up on it, with the toe of one foot searching blindly for a hold so minute and sloping that a sugar cube could not be trusted to sit on it - well, each man to his own, but the pleasure of such climbing as we had that morning on The Cioch Nose surpasses most.

The climbing over, we made our way down the mountainside and collected our sacks from the base of the cliff.

On our way back to the car we stopped at the waterfalls we had passed a couple of hours earlier and had showers on the open hillside.

Not a bad spot to be!

When we arrived back at the little bridge by the road we brewed tea beside the river and sat once again on the hot boulders.

We looked at our watches.

It was 7.15 a.m. Time for breakfast!

The final day of the holiday was spent in Glencoe once again as we drove South.

As you stand at the entrance to the Clachaig Hotel you can stare up at the hillside opposite and see a deep cleft which rends the mountain from top to bottom.

This is the Clachaig Gully.

It is 1,735 ft long and usually, given the rainfall in that region, is wet and slimy as well as being steep.

In July of 1983, however, and in particular in the week that we chanced to be there, I doubt if even a cloud had passed over Clachaig Gully, let alone a single drop of rain.

And so Alan and I set off up the hillside to the foot of the gully, and, unroped, we continued to climb up the gully bed, easily avoiding the stream coming down.

Normally the stream is a raging torrent, and its spray, as it cascades down over a thousand foot of rock, from the dozens of waterfalls inside the gully, makes for slippery and dangerous climbing on the sidewalls and forces the climber in certain places to climb directly up the rocks under the waterfalls.

This year things were different.

At the great cave pitch we roped up and scrambled up the right hand wall then back leftwards into the gully again.

The rock was dry and it was pleasantly cool to be in the shade.

From time to time our way would take us into the sunshine where we felt the force of the sun's heat in the heatwave which Scotland was experiencing at that time. And then as we rose higher up the gully we would return to the shade and were able to scoop up cool water to drink as we climbed.

The waterfall pitches, rather than being the freezing, drenching thrutch that they usually are, were actually refreshing and enjoyable. And even though we were both fairly wet at the top we dried off very quickly in the afternoon sunshine.

Our descent to the Clachaig Hotel and the refreshment which followed marked the end of a most enjoyable week.

As I said at the start of this tale, sometimes everything just falls into place!

Walking With A Legend.

"Of course the man's a legend!" said Helmut to me as we strode together along the trail in Northern Spain. "There is nobody like him, I tell you. Nobody!"

I had met Helmut a few years before when I had been visiting Long Island, New York. I had been introduced to the stocky German-American by a mutual friend, one Dick Opsahl, with whom I had been spending a holiday walking in the Appalachians.

Now, chatting as we walked, Helmut asked me how I had come to meet the man about whom we were talking.

It had been in 1987 when I was participating in the First Everest Marathon. I had found myself at relatively short notice invited to be one of the doctors on the team going to Nepal to provide medical support to the marathon runners who were intending to run a marathon race from Gorak Shep on the Khumbu Glacier at the foot of Mount Everest to Namche Bazaar, a little village further down the valley system surrounded by big mountains.

There were about 25 runners on that occasion and my job, as a doctor, was to ensure that they remained fit and well and came to no harm, and to treat them if they became injured or ill.

My advice to them all, from the outset, was *not* to take part in so foolish an event!

Running a marathon at sea level is hard enough, but at 15,000 ft....madness!

Or so I thought.

Although the course of the Everest Marathon was downhill mainly, involving a net descent of about 4,000 ft, there were substantial parts of it that would be uphill, and in any event, what with the thin, cold air, and the remoteness of the situation, it seemed to me that it would be asking for trouble to try to run such an arduous course over ice, snow, moraine, rough boulders, rickety bridges and suchlike, with severe risk of dehydration, exposure, a nasty fall, and a hundred and one other disasters which seemed to my mind almost inevitable.

But as the group had walked slowly up the trail towards Everest basecamp, taking a couple of weeks to do the trek up into the mountains from Katmandu, we had got to know each other and I, for one, had developed an interest in the backgrounds of these runners who had come from afar to run this course, and I had grown amazed to hear their tales of endurance running events.

There was the stocky Scot who had completed many marathon events always carrying two buckets, one in each hand, which became filled with coins as the miles went on. He collected for charity. There would have been many kilograms in each hand by the end!

There was the Scottish vicar who, it appeared, seemed incapable of stopping running, so many marathons had he done.

The Naval officer in our midst had likewise done dozens of marathon events, and there were others from various countries in Europe who said they did about six or seven marathons every year.

There was a wiry young soldier who had finished one of his marathons in about two hours and twelve minutes and who habitually did times around that speed.

And then there were the Americans. They came with their tales of arduous competitive events which, quite frankly, amazed me.

There were stories of twenty-four hour non-stop running events in which each person just kept on running all the time, but was allowed to have drinks if he wanted. The idea was to see who had gone the farthest round the track at the end of the period.

One American told of his "Man Versus Horse" races over vast courses of mountains and valleys in wilderness areas of the U.S.A. in which the horses would be leading virtually all the way, but would begin to tire after about forty miles and it would be at that time that he, the "Man", would overtake and sometimes win.

There was the Iron Man, one Bill Beddor, who had competed in the Hawaiian Iron Man events in which competitors swim several miles at sea, then bicycle a hundred and twenty miles, then run a full marathon.

Bill had also taken part in forty-eight hour endurance running contests and had taken first place in one such event, completing over 160 miles in the time and beating all the other runners, many of whom had been considerably younger than him. Bill had been fifty nine years old, I think, at that time!

And then there was Dick Opsahl. He specialised in ultrathons!

These are running events involving distances over a marathon (twenty six and a half miles) and generally are either fifty mile events or (yes, you heard me right!) one hundred miles!

Not only do these races take place over vast distances, but also they are very often in the mountains, and at high altitude!

For example the "Leadville 100" which is in the Rocky

mountains of Colorado and is at an average height of 10,000 ft.

Each runner must complete the course within thirty hours....or else it does not count!

As far as I could tell Dick had done the "Leadville 100" many times, and numerous other hundred mile endurance races, as well as innumerable of the "short" fifty mile ultrathons.

It appeared almost that he did marathons as an hors d'oeuvre before breakfast!

He wore a grizzly beard and a look of determination - not surprisingly!

These endurance runners could often be identified by the fact that they were carrying water bottles in their hand and were constantly drinking.

A high fluid intake, you see, is essential to avoid dehydration at altitude or in endurance running events.

One thing that struck me was the evident satisfaction which these ultramarathon runners derived from their races, and the cameraderie which they shared with each other.

Also of note was their painstaking attention to diet; I recall how on more than one occasion I offered a bag of dried mixed fruit and nuts to a runner and he, instead of pulling out a handful and scoffing it, began picking at individual tiny particles and rejecting them saying, "Cholesterol! Never touch the stuff!"

I think he must have found some chocolate chips and little

morsels of shredded coconut in amongst the fruit and nuts.

Peculiar though such behaviour seemed to me, I had to confess that there must be something in their fanaticism because clearly they were extremely fit and had stupendous powers of endurance.

I had met up with Dick Opsahl once since that Everest Marathon in 1987 and that was when he had come to England to run in the London Marathon.

I think he had just completed the Boston Marathon when he had flown to England for the London, and the very same afternoon that he had finished the London he had caught a train from London up to Windermere and we had set off together for Scotland to meet up with my brother David and for the three of us to have a week's backpacking in Knoydart.

At that time I had been struck by the not inconsiderable amount of energy and fortitude which would have been required for a man in his middle fifties to run two marathons in a short space of time, in two different continents, and then undertake a fairly strenuous walking tour in the Highlands carrying gear and food for a week - and enduring mostly heavy rain.

But that was nothing for Dick.

And so it was that I found myself on one October's day in 1998 landing at Kennedy airport, New York, and being met by Dick who took me to stay the night at the lovely timber house in Huntington, Long Island, where he and Judy had lived for many years.

Judy had prepared trail-meals for us to carry - for we were to set off the next day to Virginia to walk a stretch of the Appalachian Trail in the Blue Ridge Mountains.

The drive to Lynchburg, Virginia, was nine hours long through delightful rural scenery. We stopped occasionally to buy fruit from wayside stalls.

In Lynchburg we stayed the night with Bernie and Helen Davis, more running friends of Dick's. Bernie's walls were festooned with trophies, gongs and medallions.

He was very thin.

Next day we rose at 5 a.m. and ate a splendid breakfast of fruit juice, porridge oats, bread and (to my surprise!) bacon and eggs before Helen drove myself and Dick up the U.S. 501 highway into the hills and deposited us just before 7 a.m. near a road bridge over the James River.

It was pitch black. We put on our headtorches, said goodbye to Helen, and left the road at a little A.T. sign where a trail led deep into the woods.

The trees closed around us as we picked our way in the dark.

The trail was easy to follow. Every so often there would be a white paint flash on one of the trees to show us the way. These reassuring paint marks exist throughout the entire 2,300 miles of the A.T. though in some places are less obvious and more infrequent.

In Winter, so I was told, when snow was blown onto the trees, it was hard to distinguish the paint marks.

But here they were every couple of hundred yards or so.

We began the day at an altitude of 250 metres above sea level and wound our way slowly uphill as the morning sunlight slanted through the autumnal trees.

It was peaceful and cool.

We passed the little Matts Creek Shelter, a small wooden lean-to, crossed a small bridge, and began to climb more steeply.

There was a ground mist which gave an eerie, sepulchral feel to the forest, but it sure was beautiful.

High on the hillside we were able to look down on the bend in the James River far below us, and as we walked on we came across places on the trail with strange names..... like High Cock Knob, which we reached around 10 a.m.

The day grew hotter as we crossed Petite's Gap and entered the Thunder Hill Wilderness.

An eagle hung in the air above us as we neared the summit of Thunder Hill, beyond which we came to the Thunder Hill shelter - a wooden lean-to just South of the summit.

Our first task was to find water.

This was a perpetual problem on the A.T. because, unlike in the hills of Britain where streams abound, here the ground was dry and streams were very few and far between. Sometimes a well would have been dug near to a hut, but more often we would have to search for water.

Inside the hut someone had written a scratchy note and nailed it to a wall. It said that water could be found three quarters of a mile from the hut, and it gave directions.

I set off having memorised the directions...."Four hundred yards left of the trail and reach a back country road. Go left along the road for another 600 yards and into the woods. See a rocky bluff on your left - and the water is just to your right."

It sounded straightforward.

But it was not quite so easy!

In the gathering gloom of the evening it was a little difficult to judge distance precisely, and there seemed to be more than one rocky bluff. And there was no sign of water anywhere.

Having spent several minutes looking around and expecting to come across a veritable stream or fountain, it was obvious there was none. So I did the only thing I could think of - I stood still and remained absolutely quiet. I strained my ears and thought I could hear a faint trickling sound. It was perhaps thirty metres off into the woods - but then again, perhaps not.

We had climbed over 1,000 metres of ascent that day and carried big packs up fifteen miles, and we were both thirsty.

I crept slowly towards the deceptive sound.

It was so indistinct that I could not be sure - but there was certainly no water that I could see.

"Dawn In The Forest"
(private collection)
from an oil painting by the author

There it was again: a little drip, drop, dropping sound, and as I parted the undergrowth I saw a small pool of dark water amongst the tree roots and fallen leaves and branches; and the next hour I spent catching tiny drops in the water bottles I had brought. The pool was so shallow that I could not immerse the bottles.

Eventually, with the two bottles full, I returned to the shelter in near darkness.

Dick cooked us a meal and we lit a fire in case bears came in the night.

Next day we ate oatmeal porridge and black coffee with no sugar. Dick only takes sugar when running a hundred miles!

We headed South through the woods and over Apple Orchard Mountain where there is a large radar tracking station on its 4,225 ft summit.

We wandered through endless autumnal woods whose colours were yellow, green, red and brown.

The trail was easy to follow and white daubs appeared reassuringly on trees at approximately every three hundred paces.

The day's walk was 10.9 miles and it took us up and down till we reached the Black Rock viewpoint where we drank our water and ate nuts and raisins.

The water had to be filtered because Giardia is endemic in the woods. Some people use iodine to purify their water but we used Dick's Katadyn filter pump which, reputedly, was capable of sucking water straight up from a sewer and into your mug to drink - but we didn't try that!

Each time we passed a little creek with a trickle of water we'd stop and spend a half hour doing some more filter pumping to refill our bottles.

We had till then seen nobody else on the trail but later that afternoon there were two hikers headed North, and our paths crossed.

After a long descent through the woods we reached Bryant Ridge Shelter, which, according to the map, was situated in the Jellystone National Park.

Hey! There really is such a place!

We were cooking cous-cous in the shelter as darkness fell, and Southwind arrived.

Each thru-hiker (that means someone hiking the whole 2,300 miles of the A.T.) has a trail-name, and this preacher from Pennsylvania strode rapidly down through the trees towards us and introduced himself as Southwind.

He walked alone.

He averaged twenty-six miles a day - that means some days he may do a bit less, but others he did *more.* Try keeping that up for a few months, day after day, on your own. Even in flat country that is some achievement, but in mountainous terrain, carrying your own food, and having to locate water from time to time, that is a remarkable record.

Southwind, like a lot of thru-hikers, had someone back home who was willing, every several days, to post a box of food and other items to a pre-ordained destination somewhere on the trail.

Back in his home there would have been a room full of cardboard boxes prepared in advance with carefully selected supplies, likely numbered from one to fifty, and the arrangement would probably have been to keep sending those boxes on agreed dates to their destinations, and only to vary the schedule if the hiker sends back a message from some remote farmstead saying, "Sore foot. Delay schedule by one week," or some similar instructions.

It didn't look as if Southwind would be varying any schedule!

He carried no stove. He walked in trainers, not boots. He did not carry a stick. And he was totally vegan, eating not even milk, butter, cheese, eggs or fish - no animal product whatsoever.

In his pack he had a large plastic container of oatmeal and grain and into this each morning he would add water so that by the day's end the mixture had been sloshing around for many hours on his back and was sort of "cooked".

This he would eat with his little spoon (lightweight, and with cut-off handle).

He was lean.

Dick and I made a fire in a clearing beside the hut and the three of us sat on logs in the dark and listened to Southwind and his tales of adventures from Mount Katahdin in Maine all the way down to the Blue Ridge Mountains in Virginia.

Back up the trail a couple of days he had come across black bears just North of the James River.

"Yes," he confirmed, "You really must never get between a mother bear and her cubs!"

Also he'd nearly trodden on a rattlesnake several days back.

And spookiest of all was encountering bow-hunters in the woods. These are men who disappear into the woods for days on end and camouflage themselves and lurk silently in concealment, armed with powerful bows and arrows to shoot deer like Red Indians used to.

I felt privileged to sit there in the flickering firelight with the tall pines surrounding us, with shooting stars tearing streaks through the sky above us, and listening to Southwind's tales.

The next morning we were up at 6.30 a.m.

Southwind ate a black seed biscuit and silently slipped into the dark woods before sunrise, on his way to Georgia.

Dick and I set off a little later and were no doubt a little slower!

After a few miles we came to Jennings Creek and met another thru-hiker by the name of Forder. He too was headed South.

As the morning sun lit the foliage it was like walking under a ceiling of fairy lights. I stopped for several minutes to take a few photos and lost sight of Dick ahead.

After several minutes I decided to catch him up but after walking quickly for a quarter of an hour I could not see him. So I put on a spurt and walked as fast as I could, but still no sign of him.

It was uphill here and I kept up the speed, pushing myself hard for a few miles till the trail flattened out, but there was no sign of Dick and I wondered where on earth he could have got to.

I recollected an intersection on the trail a long way back and I wondered if he might have taken a wrong turning there. Or perhaps he was ahead of me?

But after a short time during which I was wondering what would be the best course of action for me to take, he appeared on the trail behind me a few yards away. He had indeed taken a wrong turn but then, realising his mistake, had walked as fast as he could uphill to see where I was!

The trees there are so dense that I had heard no sound of him approaching even though he had been blowing his whistle constantly, and both he and I had had a range of vision of no more than thirty or forty metres through the woods.

Well, I am not a slow walker, at least I don't think I was at that time, but Dick, sixteen years older than me and with just as heavy a pack as mine, had been able to catch up with me on a steep hill over two or three miles!

Maybe I should become a vegan!

The track flattened out as we reached the Blue Ridge Parkway –

a road winding through the mountains. We followed the road for a few hundred yards and saw small herds of deer in the woods alongside.

Soon we came to Bobblet's Gap Shelter - a distance of 11.7 miles from Bryant Ridge - and we met two other thru-hikers heading South, but they were going on another seven miles to the next hut.

The two stayed to chat for a while.

I was amazed to hear that they had no special dietary requirements but were willing to eat almost anything!

As Dick and I cooked a meal that night three youngsters arrived at the hut. They were two lads and a girl, mostly students, who had fallen in with each other several days back and were taking care of each other. It was nice to meet them.

In the months they had spent on the A.T. They had met all sorts of people and situations and they remarked that it was invariably poor people who proved to be the most hospitable to thru-hikers on the trail. Wealthy folk didn't help much, they said.

They told amusing stories of how when gear wore out there was an unwritten recognition on the part of manufacturers to supply A.T. hikers with new replacement gear promptly and free of charge.

From all that they said, it sounded as if they made full use of this arrangement.

I began to inspect my own gear for signs of wear.

The three youngsters had also met Southwind and they said that he was the fastest thru-hiker anyone had ever heard of. His reputation appeared to have spread North and South along the A.T.

After yarning the evening away beside the fire we turned into the lean-to and slept.

Next morning after oatmeal porridge and black coffee Dick and I set off in a lovely fresh morning with bright blue skies. We walked through woods for several miles till we came to the Wilson's Creek Shelter.

The leaves on all the trees shone like light bulbs.

In the late afternoon we reached the Fullhardt Knob Shelter, situated near the top of a wooded hill.

Oaks and cherries and maples and pines surrounded us.

The sun fell down through the trees and set them ablaze with red and orange light, till darkness arrived and we settled down to a meal beside a log fire outside the shelter.

In the skies over the hills on the opposite side of the valley I could see a display of shooting stars which made me feel both elated and very small, all at the same time - if you know what I mean.

We talked of this and that and Dick told of how he had started running whilst employed at Grumman in New York, and how he had persevered and found within himself the resources to do ultramarathon distances, and how he had organised and taken part in a whole series of daily marathons for Russian and American runners throughout an entire fortnight in order to foster international friendship, and how he was planning to complete four major hundred mile mountain endurance races all in one year.

It was when I began yawning that we both turned in to the lean-to and slept.

Our packs were lighter now and it was easier going downhill through the woods next morning.

Dawn in the forest was something special.

The air had a quality one cannot describe.

As we approached the little village of Troutville, Virginia, the sun rose and the ground flattened out beneath our feet.

A dead racoon lay on the side of the road.

As we entered the town an apple farmer sold us bags of apples from his farm sheds. He told us to sample them first before buying and so between us we had eaten almost a dozen different kinds of apple trying to decide which ones we liked best before eventually buying a big bag each for a few cents.

We reached the T.A. (Truckstops of America) which is a big complex where trucks pull in and drivers get out to stretch their legs and fill up their colossal vehicles with hundreds of gallons of fuel at a few cents a gallon.

Each truck is the home of its driver, and some are literally as big as a home, being almost fifty yards long and having huge polished exhaust pipes sticking up into the air. Their sirens make a deep bellowing noise.

One of these trucks was a "Travelling Chapel" and the trucker/preacher had his name and religion emblazoned on the sides...... "Come to Jesus. Get married here! Get baptised inside! Get Religion!"

Inside the T.A. Dick and I bought luxury showers using our credit cards.

Then we headed for the restaurant where all my ideas of becoming a vegan disappeared in an instant with the sight of their self-service canteen.

There were displays of roasted meats, fish, salads, vegetables, variously cooked potatoes, rice dishes, soups, pastas.........and we had about two hours to kill whilst waiting for Helen to come and pick us up.

I confess Southwind would have been disappointed in my behaviour as I returned to the self-service bar for a second helping.....or was it a third?

One small occurrence typified the bounteous nature of the restaurant - it was the waitress who constantly came round to ask if everything was all right (how could it have been otherwise?) and when she asked me if I wanted a small or a large coffee I replied, "Large, thank you," whereupon she reappeared with a thermos flask containing a couple of litres of black coffee and another containing a litre of hot milk and placed them on the table for me!

We sat sipping hot coffee and burping contentedly surrounded by truckers wearing cowboy hats and Durango boots: as my diary records.....what a country!

After a couple of hours of indulging ourselves in what really was one of the best and most cost effective feeds I've ever experienced, Helen arrived from Lynchburg to collect us.

The drive to Troutville had taken her about an hour and when at last she arrived at the T.A. truck-stop I think we were almost halfway through the thermos of coffee!

On the way back to Lynchburg Dick announced that he had a surprise in store for me.

"Hey Jan," he said, (New Yorkers say Jan, not John), "I gotta treat for you. Tomorrow we're entered for the Mountain Masochist Ultrathon."

"How wonderful," I replied, although perhaps I didn't put it quite like that. I feared something sinister was afoot.

A few questions revealed my worst fears: Dick had entered both of us for the fifty mile Mountain Masochist race which took place in the Blue Ridge Mountains to the North of the James River and, what's more, the event was tomorrow!

That night at Bernie's, the house filled up with thin strangers from various parts of the U.S.A. They had been training for many months for the event and were full of tales of runs and marathons and ultrathons.

Their jerseys were testimony to their achievements, listing dozens of events which they had entered and survived.

It was like being back on the Everest trail again.

"Bernie," I said, "Tell me, do you run every day?"

"Why no, John," he replied. "I certainly do not. Not every day, at least. I remember there was a day back in October 1988 when I didn't go for a run that day."

There came a shout from Helen in the kitchen; "It was September the fourteenth! And it was 1987. That was the day you didn't run!"

I finished my meal thoughtfully.

I remember being woken up at some totally unacceptable hour on the morning of Saturday October 16th 1998 and sitting down in front of a huge breakfast prepared by Bernie and Helen, alongside several other bodies - then we bundled into a car and drove for an hour up into the hills with the car stereo playing the sound track to the film "Chariots of Fire" .... as if these guys needed any encouragement.

It was freezing and pitch black still at 6.30 a.m. when two hundred and fifty runners including myself heard the gunshot which set us off into the darkness.

Before long I found myself on my own (no, you've guessed it wrong - not out in front of everybody, but at the back!).

As the various meals I had consumed in the past twenty-four hours made their presence felt and necessitated sideways excursions into the woods I became more aware of how alone I was.

Still, Dick had said that there would be trestle tables every few miles with refreshments for the runners, and the course was well marked with strips tied onto trees every fifty to one hundred yards, so I plodded along.

The sun rose and brought warmth to the air, and that made me feel better.

I passed the first trestle table as they appeared to be packing up, and the people there gave me drinks and looked strangely at me.

After another four miles there was a second table and more people handing out drinks and things to eat. There were still no other runners in sight.

By the third or fourth table I was getting the hang of it - have a sandwich at the table, eat some crisps and maybe a couple of potatoes, and grab a power bar to munch along the way, gulp down a couple of mugs of drink, and on you go.

After another table or two I spotted some runners ahead of me. Then I passed them. Soon there were several runners behind me and more were visible in front. I chatted with each of them for a few minutes and then either they or I would move ahead slowly.

Each table had a sign saying how many miles you had done, so it was encouraging to count the miles as they grew.

The countryside was beautiful; rich wooded hills, with the trail winding all over them, often quite steeply uphill, then down again.

The day was hot and sunny. I took off my long trousers and my jersey and wrapped them round my waist.

All the folk at the tables were most friendly and I often spent far too long chatting with them and complimenting them on their display of food. This pleased them enormously, because obviously they had all gone to a lot of trouble to cook the food and carry it out so far into the countryside and set up tables. I guessed there must have been roads fairly near by, but I seldom saw one.

I was enjoying the day.

Obviously I could not possibly do more than about half the distance - it had never entered my head that I might be able to! But I thought I would keep plodding along and see how far I could get.

The regular supplies of food and drink were delicious and very sustaining and it was with surprise that I found myself passing the table which marked twenty-six miles, a marathon distance completed, and still I was plodding on, running slowly on the flat and downhill sections and generally walking on the uphill parts.

Some of the hills were quite big, and near the top of one I came to a trestle table with lots of people and much food, and as I sustained myself and chatted to the people I realised how close I was to the "cut-off" time for each table, and it was explained to me that if you did not arrive at each table by a certain time you would be cut out of the race.

It appeared that I must have been reaching every table at just about the “cut-off” time, and that I was cutting things too fine and was at risk of getting excluded.

So, less eating and more going!

There was a loop of track at about thirty miles which led over rough country and back again to the table before - the loop was about four miles I think - and I decided I had better buck up or else I would get cut out. I was able to pass a number of people on the loop , although it must have been a bit like a tortoise passing a snail!

By half way through the afternoon I was most certainly slowing down and at last I came to one table where the kind people put me out of my misery and told me that I had just missed the cut-off time. I professed disappointment (and indeed to a certain extent I was) but it was nice to stop!

There were several others who arrived within the next half hour. It appeared that had I reached that table a couple of minutes earlier I would have been permitted to continue beyond the forty-two mile table......c’est la vie!

We “cut-out” guys commiserated with each other and were told that we would be transported to the finish by a bus, which sure enough came along carrying yet more “cut-outs” from previous tables back down the trail. It seemed there were a fair number of us!

The bus dropped us at the finish where we witnessed the arrival of runners as they approached the line, some wearily and some showing surprising signs of energy.

I spotted a small figure with a grizzly beard and a look of determination running steadily towards the line and showing no sign of fatigue. It was unmistakably Dick Opsahl; and not only did he do the finish once, but he had to go back a distance and do it again for the photographers, and again for some more photographers who had missed him the first and second time - and then some more to get better angles!

He did the finish a dozen times at least!

Later that night at the prize-giving ceremony there were roars for each finisher.

The winner had done a time which was a little over six hours, I think, and I recall calculating that such a time worked out at almost nine miles an hour for fifty miles over steep and rough ground. Even on a mountain bike that would be some going! These guys sure don't mess around!

Dick chatted to friends and acquaintances about plans for more events, training schedules, diets, strategies, insoles, fluid intake, salt depletion, stretching exercises etc......the sort of topics which, I guess, ultrathon athletes talk to each other about, whilst I flaked out on a bench experiencing the pain and stiffness which was to rack me for the next couple of days.

Everybody seemed to know Dick.

Two years later I heard that he had indeed accomplished the feat of completing four 100 mile mountain races in one season. He was sixty six years old at the time he did this.

I'm not sure if anyone else has ever done four such events in one season.

And sometimes in consultations with patients in my practice in Windermere I tell them stories of what Dick Opsahl has been up to, of his long distance running, mountain climbing, trekking and exploring, and I add by way of encouragement; "And hey, guess what, Dick is only eight (or ten, or whatever) years older than you!".

And if they start telling me of their bad knee or foot or something I might go on to say, "Hey, that's no big deal; Dick Opsahl ran a marathon whilst suffering from a painful foot," or "Dick walked seven hundred miles across northern Spain only days after having treatment to a bad knee," or the one I like best is how, a few weeks after he had broken his leg whilst long distance running in Patagonia, he went to his doctor back home in the U.S.A. to get the plaster cast taken off his leg and he took with him his running shoes and kit - and he ran right out of the doctor's surgery!

I think that was *after* the cast had been removed!

By now quite a number of my patients have heard stories of Dick Opsahl!

Helmut had been right when he had said, "The man is a legend."

Episode In Kenya.

In the early part of the year 1974 I was employed as a doctor on one of the medical wards at Aberdeen Royal Infirmary when it happened that there were ward closures for some reason or other. Because of this I was asked if I had any particular wish as to how I should spend the three months of closure time, and I was able to arrange to travel to Kenya, visit my sister Alice and her family who were resident in Kenya at that time, brush up on some tropical medicine, and perhaps do some climbing on Mount Kenya.

I arrived in the village of Nyeri and, whilst staying as a guest at my sister's bungalow, where she lived with her husband at that time and their two little children Josephine and Ashley, I was able to see what went on at the local hospital.

From the bungalow one could clearly see Mount Kenya soaring into the blue sky, its summit white with snow. It rose up out of the vast plains and surrounding forests, the ground first piling up below it in the form of a steep, jungle-covered hill of perhaps twenty miles diameter, then above this the treeless areas, topped by glaciers and the twin rocky peaks known as Batian and Nelion.

I was keen to explore the mountain and asked John and Alice if they knew of anyone who would accompany me.

They suggested that I ask Hannington, the house-boy who helped in their bungalow and garden.

Out in the garden I found Hannington.

I pointed at the mountain there in the distance. It looked enticing.

"Hannington," I said, "Would you like to come with me and climb the mountain?"

"Okay," he replied.

"You'll need proper clothes," I added, wanting to ensure that our expedition was well organised; "It could be cold."

"Okay," said Hannington.

"Right ho," I said, "Will you meet me here at three o'clock?"

"Okay," said Hannington.

So off he went to get his proper clothes for our trip, and off I went to get mine.

I found for myself some boots, thick socks, gloves, a warm jacket and a rucksack, and I put a rope in it for good measure, also an ice axe.

At three o'clock I was standing in the garden when Hannington arrived dressed in a smart, dark grey suit. He wore a white shirt, a tie, smart black shoes (which he had obviously polished), and a big smile on his face. His attire suggested a lack of mountaineering experience. I paused in my tracks, suddenly disconcerted by the image which he presented to me.

He looked more as if he were off to join in some gospel choir, or about to set off for a church meeting, than to take part in an intrepid climbing expedition.

It had not occurred to me that someone who lived so near to the foot of the mountain would not know that snow was cold stuff, and that mountains were steep, and demanded more serious kit than a grey suit, white shirt, and polished shoes!

I guessed that he had not been mountaineering before.

"What ho, Hannington," I said, "I can see you've not been up the mountain before, have you? I'd better lend you some warm clothes."

So I hunted through drawers and cupboards until I had found the necessary jerseys, gloves, socks, boots etc for him, and once he was suitably dressed he looked more the part for a mountain adventure, although he seemed a bit disappointed to be wearing battered old trousers and jersey rather than his Sunday best!

"Okay?" I asked.

"Okay," came the reply, and we both grinned.

Thus we entered the Mount Kenya National Park via the Naro Moru entrance.

We had a long, steep walk in front of us. Most people who entered the Park were driven in Landrovers up the first several miles to the roadhead at a height of about 10,000 ft, but Hannington and I had decided to walk.

It would be better for our acclimatisation.

As we walked together through the forest, gaining height slowly, I probed Hannington with questions concerning the wildlife we might encounter on the trail.

He was a local and would have local knowledge.

"Lions, John," he said. "Maybe lions."

That hadn't occurred to me! But of course, we were in Africa. Lions could well be lurking nearby.

"Oh," I said, "Do you really think we'll see lions?"

"Maybe," said Hannington.

"And what precisely do we do if we see one?" I asked.

"Climb a tree pretty damn quick," came the reply.

I cast my eye around at all the surrounding trees; some were thick with thorns and obviously unsuitable for climbing, and some were of the very-tall-and-not-too-many-branches-down-below variety. They did not look possible to climb either.

"Hmmmm," I murmured, "Which tree would you climb, Hannington?"

He looked around and pointed at all the trees. "When you see lion, John, you climb nearest tree pretty damn quick!"

"Okay," I said.

We discussed the various other types of wildlife that we might encounter. They all sounded bad, but I gathered that the worst one to meet would be a buffalo.

The buffalo, apparently, is most belligerent, never timid, easily roused to anger, and has very long, sharp horns and a short, quick turning circle. He is capable of goring you even if you were to be so lucky as to evade his charge by dodging round the back of a tree.

The rhino, however, although weighing in at several tons, and having a huge, pointed horn, is apparently not so fearful a foe because it is short-sighted and if you keep still it has difficulty seeing you.

But it has excellent hearing!

It can only charge in straight lines apparently, and is not so good at swerving, so, (said Hannington), if we encountered a rhino I should keep as still and silent as possible until it was almost upon me in its charge. The chances are that with its poor eyesight it would get its aim wrong and miss me entirely, but if its charge happened to be on course then I should wait until the very last instant and suddenly leap sideways, imitating the action of a matador. Then I could nip behind an adjacent tree.

All this gave much food for thought.

Thus engaged in conversation we picked our way up through the forest.

I was careful not to stray more than a few yards from any tree in whatever direction.

The trees were thinner once we got past the roadhead after a few hours walking - and so was the air.

So far we had not encountered wild beasts!

We climbed more steeply now as we got above the tree line and entered the Teleki Valley.

We camped for the night on the floor of the valley.

Here we came across the giant lobelia plants which are peculiar to this mountain and which look like things out of a science fiction film, standing like sentries dotted all over the valley, tall and straight.

That evening as we made our camp we heard footsteps coming downhill towards us. It was a group of natives carrying a European who, they told us, had collapsed a bit higher up the mountain and was seriously ill.

This was my first encounter with "mountain sickness", and it did not look good to see a prone body transported unconscious in this way.

Evidently there were dangers above, as well as below!

Next day the two of us made our way slowly higher up the valley.

The air was thin, and breathing was noticeably harder.

But the mountain was in sight and we could see our way up to the right as a track wound higher up the hillside towards the glaciers and, we were told, a hut.

We climbed more slowly now because of breathlessness, but eventually came to arrive at Top Hut which was at an altitude of about 15,700 ft on the border of the Lewis Glacier.

Poor Hannington had never been so cold.

Across the glacier was Nelion, the rocky peak which had first been climbed by Eric Shipton.

It looked so close.

Directly behind the hut was Point Lenana, a subsidiary peak covered with snow and rising to a height of 16,355 ft.

It looked straightforward and so Hannington and I kicked our way up the snow till we reached its summit.

There were big grins all round!

Hannington couldn't wait to get back down and tell his friends where he had been and what it had been like, and in particular how snow is actually very cold stuff!

It had been an adventure for the two of us.

It was a few weeks later that I decided to venture up the mountain for a second time.

This time an engineer called Charlie Kewin said he would come too.

He had lived in Nyeri for a while and was engaged in one of the road building projects in the countryside.

We intended to approach the mountain from the same direction, up the Teleki valley, and to climb first Nelion, then across the Gate of the Mists to the summit of Batian via the Shipton route from the Lewis Glacier.

We had with us two 9 mm ropes of 150 ft length and a few slings and karabiners and also some chocks.

First we visited the local market in the village and bought some buffalo meat which we cooked and put into our sacks.

We each had a duvet jacket, sleeping bag, and a water container.

Having notified the Park Office of our intentions and obtained permits for the climb we obtained a ride on a landrover which took us up the first several miles of track to the roadhead at 10,000ft.

From there we walked up into the Teleki valley and, turning the base of the mountain on its Southwest flank, reached Top Hut at 15,700 ft.

Here we encountered a lone Italian.

I think his name was Sergio.

He was large and round and well-equipped and he announced that he too was bound for the same route as ourselves. Could he join us, perhaps?

Why yes, we answered, and so there were three.

The route up the mountain is quite long and complex but not too difficult technically.

The summit of Nelion is at 17,022 ft which gives a little over 2,000 ft of rock climbing from the Lewis Glacier.

The altitude certainly would slow us down, and with three on a rope we would move more slowly than with two.

It would be a long day because the climb to the summit of Nelion was reckoned to take about five hours and then another couple of hours or more to reach Batian and return to Nelion.....and all this at 17,000 ft, and then the descent.

Still, the weather looked set fair.

I had been in Nyeri over a month and in all that time had scarcely seen a cloud.

We set off at the earliest crack of dawn and made our way across the Lewis Glacier in half-light. Temperatures were well below freezing.

The glacier had a set of tracks crossing it and these were easy to follow.

To our left the glacier broke away in a series of ice cliffs at the head of the Teleki Valley.

Once across the glacier we scrambled up the scree and made for the first pitch of rock and roped up at its base.

It was still very early and the cold was intense.

The guidebook described a complex route with a succession of chimneys, ledges, gendarmes and grooves with traverses rightwards and leftwards, zig-zagging up the mountain.

We climbed these as the morning advanced.

It grew hotter once the sun was up.

We climbed in pitches when it was steep, which meant that the two below would stand, belayed to the rock, whilst the leader was surmounting the difficulties above. He then would belay and bring up the next man, and then the third. The time taken for this is, of course, considerably longer than if it had just been the two of us climbing.

We came to Shipton's Cracks, about halfway up the mountain, and as I led up I became aware of clouds gathering below and around us.

Each pitch was taking too long.

"Come on, Sergio," I shouted. "We mustn't waste time."

The air grew colder and our breathing harder as we neared the 17,000 ft mark, and after some more time and struggles there we were on the summit of Nelion.

We crossed the summit and peered over to Batian, partially

obscured by clouds.

The Gate of the Mists was precisely as named: shrouded in mist. It is a narrow band of snow about 120 ft across with vertiginous drops on either side, and it forms the connection between the twin peaks.

As we prepared to make the drop of a rope's length directly onto the knife edge of snow we looked around us and saw the snow storm coming.

It was getting late and we decided we would retreat into the little tin bivouac hut which nestled on the summit of Nelion and wait until the morning to do the traverse to Batian.

Inside the shelter we crouched and brewed tea over our primus stove.

We could hear the wind howling outside.

Flurries of snow blew in through the cracks.

We slept rather uncomfortably.

I remember waking up the next morning and looking outside.

Everything had changed.

No clear blue sky. No sun. Only thick cloud, falling snow, and wind.

Very bad conditions.

We had to make haste to get down.

We abandoned the idea of crossing the Gate of the Mists.

The route we had come up had been relatively easy rock

climbing apart from three or four pitches, but it had been a complex route winding its way up the mountain, and it would not be easy trying to down-climb the same route especially in poor visibility and falling snow. Route finding would be very hard.

So we decided to abseil.

We chose our first abseil point near the edge of the chasm, knotted our two ropes together and, using a sling round a rock, passed one rope through the sling and threw both the coiled ropes out into the void.

They fell with an ominous whirring noise.

We took it in turns to lower ourselves over the edge and down into the mist using our descendeurs which are friction devices.

The first man down to the end of the ropes made himself safe to the rock using a sling or chock and karabiner and gave a shout, and was followed by the second, then the third.

One of the ropes was then pulled down, making sure that we pulled on the correct rope - the one which had the knot through the sling above; to pull on the wrong rope would simply cause the knot to jam itself in the sling.

Considerable effort was required to get the rope to move.

It moved very slowly at first and there was so much friction that we thought the rope or knot must be jammed, but once we had it flowing we kept it coming until it was nearly all through and needed no further pulling - its weight alone was sufficient to cause the other rope to rise upwards and pass through the sling above.

There was a danger that the last metre of rope would flick and catch itself on the sling or jam in a crack, and for this reason one had to take care not to pull too fast. If this were to happen a most dangerous situation would exist with almost all the rope pulled through, but with the last metre jammed above, and with three climbers perched on a ledge below, yet unable to rely on the rope to climb back up to free it. A predicament indeed!

Fortunately this did not happen.

The sling above had to be abandoned, obviously.

We retrieved both ropes and made a new abseil point with another sling.

Then we repeated the whole procedure.

Below us was 2,000 ft of steep rock.

With each abseil being at the most 150 ft we had a lot of work in front of us!

In the now heavily falling snow it would be impossible for us to climb down any of the pitches even if we were sure where we were and where each pitch was leading.

We only knew that we had a long way to go to reach the scree at the foot of the rock.

It was going to be a long, hard descent.

Each abseil grew harder as the snow fell, and as we lost height and the morning advanced this caused the temperature to rise, and, oddly enough, this made things even harder because the snow turned to sleet and began to soak us.

Our duvet jackets were good protection against cold, but hopeless in the wet.

Each abseil had its own difficulty : some had of necessity to be short because an excellent landing place would emerge when only half the ropelength had been descended....but below that was nothing but a misty emptiness; so when that happened we made that our next point of departure.

Sometimes the rope's end would be reached and still no sign of a good resting place - in which case the first man to descend would have to struggle up a bit to find a good spot for all three of us to stand on.

Sometimes we found ourselves abseiling down a chimney and with the sleet now turning to rain there was a veritable waterfall coming down onto us.

The ropes became saturated and grew heavy. This made it even harder to pull them down after us.

The knot repeatedly kept jamming and would not budge even with three of us pulling.

When this happened there was nothing for it but for me to climb back up the rock using what protection I could gain from the two sodden ropes hanging there, and invariably I would find at the top nothing to explain the cause of the jam other than just the fact that the ropes were so wet and heavy now that they were reluctant to move!

I would jiggle the ropes around and arrange them so that they were not twisted, or I would pull the knot a few metres through the sling so that it would flow more easily, then I would abseil down them to re-join the other two.

In this manner we worked our way slowly down, abseil by abseil, with constantly falling sleet or rain, and thick cloud to obscure any view, so we had no way of knowing how far below us was the scree.

We grew colder and began to shiver.

Our duvet jackets became lead weights around us, their feathers sodden.

Our fingers grew numb and rope-handling became more awkward.

It was essential not to drop a karabiner, sling, or a descendeur. This could easily have happened when standing shivering at a stance making a move to clip onto the rope.

Our supply of slings was dwindling despite cutting each one as short as possible so as to conserve our supply.

We encouraged each other to keep our spirits up. Obviously each ropelength was bringing us closer to the foot of the climb.

Having no altimeter we were unable to tell how much farther we had to go, and visibility remained atrocious.

Then it stopped raining.....and began freezing!

At the end of a very long series of arduous abseils we recognised where we were - near the foot of the first pitch that we had climbed the day before!

Above us the ropes hung down from their last abseil point and the water was turning to ice. Already the ropes were immovable, frozen.

They had to be left there.

Night was approaching and the Lewis Glacier was covered with a dense layer of thick, white cloud.

Somewhere over the other side of it was Top Hut.

Its precise location was going to be hard to find because a lot of snow had fallen and obliterated all tracks on the glacier.

Once the other side of the glacier had been reached we would have to find the point of ascent to the hut; this point was, as I remembered, a sort of gap in the rock wall and moraine. You had to find the gap, go up through it, and the hut would be easy to find from there.

But finding the gap would be hard in deep snow and thick cloud and in the dark.

To our right were the ice-cliffs at the snout of the glacier - too far to our right and we would go over those!

I took a compass bearing aiming approximately halfway between where I thought the gap was and the snout. I reckoned that if we could keep to that bearing across the glacier then all we had to do was go left once across the glacier and we would be able to find the gap. But if we had made a beeline straight at the gap (or where we thought it to be) then we would not know, if on reaching the other side we found no gap, whether it lay to our right or to our left, and we could waste time searching in both directions and only become more lost.

Our bodies were by now very cold, wet, and we were all shivering badly.

We switched on our headtorches and set off in a line.

After a few minutes I looked around. Where was Sergio?

Charlie and I could not see him. We shouted, and he came into sight staggering. Behind him was a trail of objects that he appeared to be discarding. Amongst them was the primus stove - not a good idea to leave that behind!

We were all tired and very cold indeed, all of us shivering.

I picked up the primus and we went on.

As I had expected, when we reached the far side of the glacier there was no sign of the gap which I was sure I would recognise when I came across it. I had looked carefully at it the day before as we had come that way.

However the compass bearing had taken all this into account (I hoped!) and so we turned left and groped our way through the freezing mist.

After a hundred metres or so we found it - an unmistakable way up through the rocks, and above that the hut was a matter of a few minutes in front of us.

We went inside the hut and began taking off our wet clothes.

They were turning into armour plates of ice already!

The stove came in handy and we were able to heat some snow and make hot water for drinks.

I remember crawling naked into my damp sleeping bag, as did we all, and shivering convulsively for hours on end. From time to time I got up to heat more water and we all had drinks.

The convulsions of shivering were truly uncontrollable and involved all the muscles of the body. The three of us lay there, our bodies like jackhammers making a racket as we rattled about on the bunk beds.

But eventually we warmed up and rehydrated ourselves.

The following day was almost back to normal for the weather. Just a few ragged clouds remained, and fresh snow on the mountain was evidence of the storm of yesterday.

We crossed the glacier when the sun was up and retrieved our ropes which we had left hanging on the last abseil, then we made our descent down the trail.

The snow storm on the mountain had not gone unnoticed and near the bottom of the trail we met some park rangers who were on their way up to see what had become of us and they enquired anxiously after us; but as there had been nobody else on the mountain they had no further cause for concern once we had reassured them.

Having denied the mountain the pleasure of clutching our frozen bodies to its bosom, we celebrated our escape with several "Tusker baridi" - which is Swahili, I believe, for "cold beers".

The Most Beautiful Woman In France.

"And when you come in from the beach please use the shower in the garage so that you don't bring sand into the house."

"And the fridge must be switched off and emptied before you go home at the end of your holiday."

"And the water must be turned off at the tap in the garage."

"And ensure that all doors and windows are locked and the shutters pulled to when you leave the house."

"Oh yes - one final thing - don't miss seeing the most beautiful woman in France," said John to us as he handed us the keys to his house in Pyriac, Brittany. "You'll find her in La Baule!"

"Eh what?" I chipped in, my attention caught by this last remark.

It seemed somewhat out of context being included in a list of chores to do about the house.

"Yes indeed," he went on, "The most beautiful woman in the whole of France, I would say. Wouldn't you say, my dear?" he turned to his wife.

"Absolutely! No doubt about it!" said Maria. "She has a quite perfect arse."

"And her breasts are so, so ....." continued John, lost for words.

"Pert, dear," said his wife.

"Yes, pert; that's the word. So pert!"

"Wait a minute, " I interjected, "Who on earth are you talking about?"

"Well, we think she's definitely the most beautiful woman in the whole of France. She's unbelievably gorgeous. And if you're staying in Pyriac it's only a short drive to the market square in La Baule and you can't miss her."

Now he was issuing directions as if this woman of great beauty (a living creature, I could only presume) was some sort of tourist sight to be inspected, like a monument or art gallery!

Annie and I were intrigued by all this.

We had just arranged to rent their house for a fortnight, and we were shortly to set off with two friends, Norman and Rachel, for a holiday in Brittany, and now we were being told in a very matter-of-fact manner that there was, in the market square of La Baule, the most beautiful woman in France.

Not merely a very attractive lady, not indeed a right corker - but quite simply the most beautiful woman in the whole of France.

John and Maria were adamant!

Annie was beginning to give me sidelong glances however, so I merely asked in an offhand sort of way, along with checking the directions for finding their house, where this apparition could be seen.

“You’ll find her in the market place in La Baule. Amongst the oysters!” said John grinning.

And then they went.

Several days later and we were on one of the charming beaches near Pyriac enjoying a spot of snorkelling and beach boules and a snack when I blurted out to Norman, “Hey Norman, do you want to go into La Baule and watch the England v Brazil world cup game on TV? There’s a bar in the market place and it’s got a TV. We could go and see the match.”

“Sure thing,” said Norman.

And the next morning as we sat watching the defeat of England on the TV in the Bar “M” in the market square in La Baule I told Norman what John had said about how the most beautiful woman in France is to be found in the market square....only a few yards from where we sat.

"Let us go shopping in the market place," said Norman, his curiosity aroused.

So we sauntered over to the stalls where throngs of people were buying and selling.

Markets in France are vibrant, colourful sights, where one can find all sorts of interesting things.

Together we roamed the stalls, our eyes not only on the produce but also on the traders behind the stalls.

"What about the aubergines and artichokes?" I asked.

"Not bad," said Norman, "But past their best. Hey - what about the lobsters and crayfish?"

"Mmmm....quite attractive. But surely not the most beautiful in France!"

"Take a look at the wet fish stall. Now *that's* a bit of all right, don't you think?"

"Say," said Norman, his eyes hovering somewhere over the sea bass and the red mullet, "What do you reckon to *that?*"

"Maybe," I replied, "But I'm not sure. She's kind of older than one would expect. Could be her; maybe."

"Definitely not the brie and camembert," we both agreed.

And so we walked around the market place filling our bags with fruit and vegetables and other delicious produce to take home whilst debating the relative merits of each stall-holder.

When we got home we told Annie and Rachel of our morning.

More sidelong glances!

There was one particular item, purchased from a market stall, which everybody especially enjoyed. It was a Tarte de Bretagne - a sort of round flat cake with rum and almonds in it. It was delicious.

We had bought it from a little stall owned by one Freddie Braun who had told us that he was originally from Switzerland but had settled in La Baule.

He specialised in making these Tartes de Bretagne, and he was a veritable chatterbox, delighting in practising his English to the exclusion of all else.

He loved a conversation to such an extent that, when in full flow, he was oblivious of other customers holding out hands with money in vain attempts to purchase his cakes from him, and he would tell us of all his friends in England and where he had visited.

"Oh, I am so sorree zat you av lost ze match wiz Brazil. Eeet ees a great peety. I am sinking zat England will be ow you say ze winners, but eet ees not to be!"

And he would wave away a potential customer and give himself more elbow room to enable him to expound on the merits of the various teams remaining in the World Cup.

Anyhow, we had enjoyed meeting Freddie and had especially enjoyed one of his cakes.

Our holiday continued pleasantly with trips here and there, plenty of relaxation, and on the penultimate day we decided to return to La Baule and visit its market once again, and possibly buy another of Freddie's gateaux.

This time Rachel and Annie were with us, to keep an eye on us and to inspect the delights of the market place.

We looked at old books, hats, flowers, the various fish counters, garden ornaments, well-stocked shellfish stalls, the plentiful crabs and lobsters, and after a while we found ourselves at Freddie Braun's stall once again.

"Freddie," I said, "Your tarte was delicious," and, this time with an audience of four, Freddie was off again gesticulating with both arms and telling us stories of all his relatives, his various other commercial ventures, and his trips to other countries whilst totally ignoring other customers.

Then in a break in the conversation I chipped in, "Freddie, where is the most beautiful woman in France?"

I expected his jaw to drop, his train of thought to be interrupted, his flow of conversation to cease with a stunned and perplexed silence.

What an absurd question to ask anyhow!

But no! "Down ze road to ze right," he pointed, "and zere you will find 'er in ze leetle oyster bar about feefty metres on ze left. Now as I was saying, ze favourite place where I like to go when I am wiz my friends in Eengland is ....."

"Hey, hold on a mo, Freddie," I said, "What is all this about the most beautiful woman in France? I didn't really expect you to have a clue what I was talking about."

"Yes, I would say, she ees probably, no definitely ze most beautiful woman in France. I cannot seenk zat zere could be anyone more beautiful zan she. She ees in ze leetle oyster bar wiz ze large blue sign above ze door. Zere are often many people zere. I seenk you will agree when you see 'er."

Intrigued, we headed off down the busy little road which was packed with market stalls on either side.

And there, after about fifty metres, and on our left was indeed a small but expensive-looking oyster bar where well-heeled clientele sat and sipped chilled glasses of white wine and sucked on oysters.

Some of the men were of the macho-disco type with a gold medallion nestling in chest hair revealed through open shirt front, and gold dangling at the wrist.

Some were of the shiny silk suit and expensive shoes type, having left their yachts, no doubt, moored in some port nearby.

The women were of various sorts also; some extremely bronzed and heavily made-up and with expensive dark glasses with a dash of gold at the corners of the frame.

Others were younger and fashionably dressed in chic couture or whatever it is called in France; there were plenty of good-lookers around, but who was the most beautiful? And why, when asked about "the most beautiful woman" was there so much certainty as to who it was, and where she was to be found?

It was most mysterious.

And was this beautiful lady supposed to be the owner, or a customer?

Having spent a few moments perusing the scene and still being undecided, I at last went inside the oyster bar wondering if she might perhaps be serving at the bar.

It was dark inside.

It took a few moments for my eyes, having been out in the bright sunshine, to become accustomed to the dark interior.

There behind the bar was a stout man with a large moustache.

A plump serving girl bustled past bearing trays of empties.

"M'sieur?," said the barman to me.

"Er, um, oh, well," I coughed, unable to think of anything intelligible to say at that precise moment.

"Can I 'elp M'sieur?" continued the barman.

"Well, I, er...." then throwing all caution to the wind, "Where is the most beautiful woman in France?"

"Ah, M'sieur," said the barman, "Eet ees Thursday today. Today she ees not 'ere!"

I gulped, and turned to face some sidelong glances from the others.

Bad Crow Days.

I looked up from where I was sitting at the kitchen table and shouted, "Come in!"

I was having lunch and it was strange to hear someone knocking at a window.

Why didn't they come to the front door?

There it was again.

I got up from the table and went through to see who it was.

Nobody was there!

That's odd, I thought, but I sat down and got on with my lunch.

Whoever it was will surely come round to the back door, or else it cannot have been important.

It was the Spring of 2000, and I thought nothing more of the event until the same thing happened the next day.

Once again I heard a knocking at a window.

This time I went round all the windows and I also went outside and had a good look around, but I was perplexed when I could find nobody.

The next time it occurred was only a short while later and this time I pinpointed the location of the knocking and went into the right room straight away.

There was a big, black crow tapping ferociously at a window.

It flew off the instant it saw me.

Now I have often come across small birds tapping at their reflection in a window; they seem to do it in the Spring rather than at any other time of year, and I guess it is a territorial gesture.

Perhaps they think that their reflection is another bird come to threaten them, so they peck at it in an assertive manner.

I have seen this sort of thing with robins, especially.

But this was a big crow.

You could say, in fact, it was a monster crow, because it was certainly one of the biggest I'd ever seen.

Over the next several days I became familiar with the sound of it tapping on the windows and at first this amused me, but after a while it got on my nerves.

It was a most insistent noise, very loud, and it continued for a long time, perhaps forty-five seconds at a time, with an occasional pause to make you think it had stopped, only to start up again.

Worst of all the crow started his tapping early in the morning, so at 4 a.m. there would be this loud rapping which would wake me up.

It would start at one window, then there would be a long gap of maybe half an hour, and then it would start again at another window.

Every time I ran through to the sitting room, or the study, or one of the bedrooms and if I saw the creature pecking at the window, it would see me first and be off in a flash.

After a week or two of this the experience irritated me immensely.

The wretched bird had clearly got into a bad habit, but it was so quick off the mark that each time it saw me it was gone in a split second.

We have a front door with a glass section in it, and the crow started to attack this too.

In fact we have quite a number of windows in the house, and the Bad Crow (for so we began to call it) would go round and round attacking almost all of them throughout the day.

In the early hours of the morning, just as dawn was breaking, and when we would normally be fast asleep, he started doing this every day.

It got so that I would wake up suddenly in anticipation of the tapping noise, just as dawn was beginning to break.

When I was home having some lunch, he would be there either rapping at the door or windows, or else perched ominously, like an extra in Alfred Hitchcock's film, on a tree branch looking at the house.

And in the evenings too, there he would be.

Once, after Annie and I had been away for a few days, we returned home and found a pile of bird shit on one of the window ledges, and even some bloodstains on the window, and I also saw that the windscreen wipers on my car had been chewed up and partially ripped off.

And then I spotted that the sealant compound around all the windows had been pecked at, and in some places there were substantial gaps where it had been torn away.

Something had to be done.

First I made a phone call to the buildings insurer and discussed the problem, only to learn, as I had feared, that a carrion crow destroying the fabric of the house is classified as a vermin attack, and this is specifically excluded from the insurance cover for the cost of repairs.

I phoned a friend and asked if I could borrow his airgun.

I don't know whether any of you have ever read any of Jim Corbett's books, but you really should!

Jim Corbett lived in Northern India in the early part of the twentieth century and became renowned for his prowess in hunting down and shooting man-eating tigers.

The man-eating leopard of Rudraprayag is a classic tale in which Jim Corbett pits his wits against a ferocious leopard that has killed a hundred or more villagers.

It takes Jim many months and a multitude of adventures before he rids the countryside of the killer leopard. It is an amazing story and I heartily recommend it.

"Right," I said to myself, "This crow should be no problem!"

And so, armed with a powerful .22 air rifle, I decided to get rid of this troublesome crow.

I kept the gun and a tin of pellets close at hand, and when I heard the tapping I would go quickly and silently out the back door and creep, gun in hand, around the house towards the window being attacked, imitating (or so I thought) the actions of Corbett!

Tap, tap, tap, went the Bad Crow, and I could hear him still at it as I came to the corner of the building.

Very slowly and quietly I began to look round the corner.

Within a fraction of a second the bird was off.

However quietly I went, he would hear or see me before I could get a fix on him.

It was as if he had eyes in the back of his head, literally.

How was it possible for him to be pecking away so ferociously with his beak pointed at the window, and at the same time to see me as the tip of my nose came around the house about ten to fifteen metres away and behind him?

I tried the "rush" approach – jumping fast around the corner, and taking aim to fire – but if I did that he would be sixty yards away and up in a tree by the time I could get the gun up to my shoulder – he was so quick!

The slow and stealthy approach seemed likely to be more successful, but even that did not work.

Sometimes I just poked the very tip of the gun around the corner, only a centimetre, and he would be off like a rocket.

It was uncanny.

Clearly I was not going to get him that way!

He had a few favourite windows that were suffering more than the rest; you could see how the sealant was disappearing from these in great chunks as the days went on.

So I rigged up some very fine nylon fishing line across one of these windows to try to entrap him.

I spun a sort of web of virtually invisible, very thin line which I had knotted into a net, and I let it hang loosely across one of his favourite windows so that if the bird were to try to land on that window sill he would surely get tangled in the net, and then I would get him!

But no! He just did not go to that window.

He went to all the others instead!

Then I tried tying a single line across each of several window sills, just about six inches above the sill, in the hope that this would thwart his ability to land on the sill. But it did not seem to stop him at all, and there are so many windows that he just paid more attention to others.

I put objects on the sills, mousetraps even, but to no avail.

This was a cunning crow!

I phoned friends for advice – and I must say I got lots of interesting suggestions – most of which I did try.

"Teddy bears," said one person. "Put teddy bears inside every window looking out. The crow will think these are humans or animals and will be frightened away."

We did not have enough teddy bears in the house, so had to approach other friends in order to increase our stocks.

Having acquired sufficient teddy bears and dolls we placed them inside every window staring out.

I don't know what the postman thought of all this!

But it had no effect on preventing the crow!

He was not frightened by any of this.

I picked up, once again, the writings of Jim Corbett; surely he would have something of value to say.

He would spend many a night sitting astride a tree branch in the Indian jungle waiting silently for a man-eater to come, lured by a goat kid that Jim had staked out beneath the tree.

Then he would fire a single bullet between the tiger's eyes as the beast sprang to attack.

Or he would build a machan (a cunningly camouflaged hide) and conceal himself in it for hours, or even days on end, then make his kill with a single shot.

And so I built a sort of hide; it was a large frame of wood and fencing that stuck around the corner of the house, and it was camouflaged with bits of grass and weeds, and it had a hole in the middle through which I could take aim.

When the crow was attacking the window nearest to my hide I would creep up very quietly behind the screen and slowly and silently poke the tip of the rifle through the hole and take aim ..... but the bird was gone!

Once again, he seemed able to see the very tip of the rifle even as I had just begun to poke it through the hole!

This happened several times and was most frustrating.

And so I got out the tent and located it in the best position, not too far from the window he was most likely to attack, and not too close.

At first it was evident that he did not like the presence of the tent, because he would go round the other side of the house and start his tapping there, but after a while he became used to the tent, and when I saw that he had begun to ignore the tent, and that he would be pecking away at the window nearest to it, I placed myself inside the tent, and, like Jim Corbett, decided to sit and wait, gun in hand.

Time passed and I imagined myself in the jungles of India, awaiting the arrival of a man-eater.

I had the flap of the tent already ajar so that I would have to make no movement at all other than raise the rifle to my shoulder.

I kept well back inside the tent so that such a small movement would be unnoticed by the Bad Crow.

The night passed.

Owls hooted. Things shuffled about outside.

I kept as still as I could and tried not to sneeze, cough, or clear my throat.

My admiration for Jim Corbett's ability to remain silent and in one place increased no end. It was far harder than I had thought!

Come the dawn my sense of anticipation increased because I knew it would not be long before the crow came and started his attack.

There he was!

I could hear him clearly tapping away....but at the other side of the house!

Curses!

I tried two tents....one on each side of the house, but he merely visited other windows that were not within view from either tent.

The creature was mocking me!

Each morning when I went into work I felt more exhausted.

I tried the Yellow Pages, and made contact with local companies who called themselves Pest Control Specialists.

I rang them all one by one, but none of them had ever heard of a crow which attacked windows, and they had no suggestions....until I came to one agency: "Ace Pest Control", located well inside Yorkshire, about forty miles from where we live, but here I struck it lucky.

"Ace" was a young gamekeeper who, having recently been made redundant, had set up his own agency, and he knew straight away what to do. He was familiar with the problem of rogue crows attacking windows. He said that in all probability it is the chemicals in the sealant around the glass which gives the crow a buzz, so to speak, and that the crow becomes addicted to the compound.

"You need a Larsen trap," he said with confidence.

"What's that?" I asked.

"I'll bring one round," he replied, and, as good as his word, he came the next day.

The Larsen trap was a large wire cage about 4 ft by 2 ft by 2ft, and it was divided into two cube-shaped cages by a wire partition down its middle.

Each half had a trap-door made out of wire, and in one of the boxes was a live carrion crow sitting on a perch. He was the "call bird," so-named because it was his presence and his cawing that would attract the Bad Crow into the second (empty) box.

This second box had a wire trap-door which was held open by a stick pushing hard against a strong spring. If the stick is removed the spring snaps the door shut very suddenly.

The key to the whole contraption is that the stick, which is a short piece of half inch dowel, is actually already broken into two pieces and these pieces simply press end-to-end against each other.

The stick looks solid, but it is only the force of the spring that holds it pressed together.

When the Bad Crow sees the contraption located invitingly somewhere in the garden and observes the call bird just sitting there on its perch, he thinks, "Grrr! (or Caw!….or perhaps it should be Cor!) there's a pesky rival right here in *my* patch. I'm going to fly down onto that bit of dowel which will do nicely for me to perch on whilst I give him a good seeing to!"

And then, as you will already have anticipated, the Bad Crow lands on the dowel, the dowel breaks apart into its two separate pieces, the spring pulls the trap-door shut, and Bingo! You have him!

So the trap was set up in an open part of the garden and the call bird was kept fed with cat food.

Inside the house we awaited events.

Nothing happened all the rest of the day and we went to bed.

Next morning I was up early to spy out of the window to see what we had.

And there, to my joy, were *two* black carrion crows – one being the call bird, and the other, obviously, being the Bad Crow!

Yippee! I ran over and quickly despatched the Bad Crow.

At that time of the early morning there are often a few crows to be seen perched aloft in the trees, so I danced around the garden shouting to them and waving my trophy.

"Ha!" I shouted, "I've got the blighter!"

I was overjoyed. The past several weeks had been really very trying and now it was all over.

After making a few circuits of the garden I placed the dead body on a fence post as a visible sign to teach the other crows a lesson.

I got the impression they were actually looking at me and even discussing amongst themselves. They shifted uneasily up in the high branches.

That morning I picked up the phone and rang Ace.

He was not in, but there was an answering machine, so I left a message saying I'd caught the Bad Crow and would return the Larsen trap that afternoon.

So I took him back the trap, and the call bird inside it, of course, and the first thing that Ace said to me I found slightly unnerving:-

“Are you sure it is the right crow?”

It had never entered my head that it could be anything other than the Bad Crow.

I went home pensively.

For three or four days nothing happened, and my confidence that I had caught and killed the right bird grew.

Then it started again; I couldn’t believe it!

Tap, tap, tap, tap.... early one morning.

Aaaarrgh! The Thing was back again!

Thoughts entered my head – Had I killed the wrong crow? Which one was the Bad Crow? Was there more than one Bad Crow?

By this time the story of all this was around the neighbourhood and I was able to get help from a more local gamekeeper, Stan, who also had a Larsen trap, and who kindly came round with it.

We set it up, once again with a call bird already inside. His name was Boris. We prepared to wait.

However Stan was less optimistic.

“Crows are very clever birds,” he said, “Very clever indeed. They have eyes in the back of their head, and are probably the most intelligent of birds.”

“They know the difference between a walking stick and a gun; so if I were to walk in that field with my stick, the crows would fly around quite happily. But if I were to have my gun under my arm, they would disappear.”

"Even if I were to hold my gun in the manner of a stick, they can tell!"

"So now you've killed one bird with a Larsen trap they'll know about Larsen traps, and they'll not come near, likely."

"Oh dear," I said, "I hope they have short memories and soon forget about Larsen traps."

"Not so," said the gamekeeper. "Crows have very good memories. Moreover they talk to each other and if one of them has a narrow escape he'll sit up in the branches explaining it to his friends and soon they'll all know about Larsen traps and how best to avoid them!"

Things did not look good.

We set up the trap, however, and I kept Boris supplied with cat food, and very contented he seemed – but there was no sign of the Bad Crow going anywhere near the trap, although the window attacks did continue.

I kept the airgun ready to hand inside the kitchen, and I also kept the inside doors of the house open so that I could the more easily identify which window was being attacked.

One day I heard the tapping coming from the North side and I knew this was the spare bedroom.

I crept silently down the corridor, gun in hand, and there I could see him battering away at the outside of the bedroom window. I had him in my sights, and what's more, he had not seen me!

I was in the dark of the corridor and was aiming straight at him from no more than about twelve feet.

But the thought crossed my mind that the lead slug would hit the inside of the window at an angle and might not, therefore, do its job of killing the bird on the outside. Perhaps the slug would only break the window and not even harm the bird, and then I would have a broken window to repair.

For a full five seconds these thoughts went through my mind and I stood with my finger on the trigger and the Bad Crow in my sights.

Then he saw me. Our eyes met.

For a second he stared at me and I looked back into the blackness of his evil eye, and then he was off.

However, after several days the Larsen trap did in fact catch another carrion crow – but this time, although I dispatched the crow, I was careful not to prance around the garden waving the corpse for other crows to see, so I buried it quietly.

Stan came round from time to time to see what was happening.

Sometimes he brought his shotgun and would give a blast or two at a passing crow.

He told me once again how clever crows are, but added that they are not good at counting.

"What do you mean?" I asked.

"Well," he said, "If two men walk across a field into a copse of trees and stay there for a while, then if only one man walks back across the field, the crows seem unable to know that there's still one of the two men remaining in the copse. And that's a trick we sometimes use to our advantage. The crows reckon the men have gone home, but the one who stays behind in the copse has a gun and can get a good shot when the crows come over."

Then I spotted a very big, black carrion crow looking down at the Larsen trap which was placed strategically in the garden.

The sitting room window was kept ajar and the airgun was lined up and already loaded, balanced on a cushion and pointing at the trap.

The gun was several feet inside the house so that the barrel did not protrude outside the window, so that no movement would give away my intentions.

I had seen the film "The Day of The Jackal," and I had noted how the Jackal had positioned his gun well inside his room so as to take a shot at de Gaulle, and I was going to get this crow!

The curtains were drawn, but not fully, so that it would be possible for me to get behind the gun and fire it at the trap without my movements (I hoped) being detected.

I took careful aim.

The big crow flew down and landed on the other side of the trap.

It was not possible for me to shoot when it was on the other side, so I waited.

It paced back and forth but always remaining on the other side.

Then it leapt onto the top of the cage and started flapping wildly at the call bird.

The crow would not keep still and I did not know if it intended to land on the piece of dowel or not. The way it was behaving one might almost think that it knew not to land on the dowel!

After several seconds I could wait no longer.

I fired and hit it square on.

I heard the thunk as the slug hit home – but the wretched crow just flew straight off!

That was the end of all the tapping and tearing at the windows.

The Bad Crow so far has never come back.

I repaired all the windows – it took a few days to do that.

I returned the Larsen trap to Stan and I told him what I had done.

"They have a skeleton like armour plating," said Stan. "Often, even with a .22 rifle – not an airgun – they can survive a direct hit, so strong are their bones. You really have to be very lucky to kill one with an airgun."

But sometimes we hear, a few hundred yards away, the insistent cawing of what sounds like a very aggressive crow across the road and over a field, and I remember how in the Spring of 2000 I struggled for about eight weeks to outwit that Bad Crow.

There is just one postscript to this story.

We went down to visit my sister Alice in South Wales one

weekend soon after all this, and Annie and I were sleeping in the guest bedroom.

Above the bed was a skylight window in the ceiling.

The ceiling was quite low.

I was fast asleep in bed when dawn came that summer morning and I was awoken suddenly to a startling noise which brought terror to my heart!

TAP, TAP, TAP, TAP .... and I looked up and there, directly above my head, was this skylight being attacked by a big, black carrion crow!

But it couldn't have been the same one!

Could it?

Artist Asleep On A Beach.

I filled in the application form and sent it off in the post.

It had said that Erik Gleave, artist, was willing to give tuition to small classes of students, and he invited those interested to apply.

I was trying to rekindle my interest in painting and was wanting to improve my skills.

For several years I had been prompted by my brother, David, who had kept suggesting to me that I should do some painting.

"Go on," he had said, "You used to paint many years ago. Remember that great holiday we had up in Scotland when we were touring around camping, and you did several paintings and I fished all the time? Do some more. It would be good for you."

Now the fact that David had such evident talent as a Scottish watercolourist was partly an encouragement, but also somewhat daunting for me because I fully expected that my own efforts would be hopeless by comparison.

So for many years I procrastinated.

Then one day Norman Lang, the retired Natwest bank manager in Bowness, had given me a good talking to, and it was clear to everybody that Norman had a lot of fun painting watercolours, so when he encouraged me I at last decided to have a go.

I took my first painting up to show to Norman.

I was as proud as Punch.

"Brilliant! That's super, John, really great," he had said, and we had both laughed uproariously; but from then on I had often called round to show Norman my efforts and he would show me his, and the compliments would flow back and forth.

"Wow! That's really good!"

"Hey! I really like that!"

"Brilliant, that one!"

"Yours is fantastic!"

"No, yours is far better than mine!"

For boosting self-confidence and raising one's morale it was a great way of spending a spare hour, and the mutual congratulation was accompanied by much laughter.

However the opportunity came for me to attend one of Erik

Gleave's courses, and this I did.

Erik's attitude to Art was dramatic, personal, powerful, and invigorating.

He said things that made one positively sit up and take notice.

He tried to make you see things in a different way, and he constantly referred to his store of illustrated Art books to show his students pictures from his favourites – Edward Seago, John Singer Sargent, Rembrandt, John Yardley, Edward Wesson, Russell Flint, Andrew Wyeth, Winslow Homer and others, in order to illustrate the points which he was making.

"Just look at that!" he would say, thumping a page or rapping it with the back of his hand; "See how he's highlighted the area off centre. Your eye just goes straight in. Bang! And just look at the texture of that brushstroke! Just one brushstroke. Wham! How does he do it?"

And he would sigh as he shook his head showing respect for these heroes of his.

He wanted his students to stop messing around with fiddly little brushes and small tubes of paint.

"Buy stacks of paper," he would say, "and then you won't feel inhibited. If you've only got a few sheets you feel as if you can't afford to waste any. Buy loads, and then you can use big brushes, big tubes of paint, put it on thickly, experiment, and it doesn't matter if you throw a lot of your work away in the end. It's all good practice. And without the inhibition you'll paint more freely. And then you'll begin to see things happen. Sometimes, just sometimes, you'll surprise yourself with what you've done and you won't throw that one away. Or maybe just a small part of one painting will have exactly the right happy accident that you couldn't possibly do again because you don't know how you've done it. Well, that's the one to keep!"

"If you try too hard not to waste materials you will stunt yourself. Be expressive. Experiment. Try different things all the time."

He was full of challenging bits of advice and he wanted his students to be Artists with a capital A.

He made me more interested not only in painting but also in visiting art galleries and looking at famous paintings, and seeing more and more works of art of all types, and I did get immense pleasure from this.

I struggled away with my own painting and took much flak from Erik for still using small brushes and little tubes of paint. When would I learn?!

He was kind enough to give me advice from time to time and although he was very much a professional, and in fact had been for many years in charge of Art in the Education Department in the North East of England, based at Newcastle-upon-Tyne, he did not get offended if I sometimes drove round to his place in Bardsea for a chat and to seek his comments, or if I phoned him for advice.

But his life took a downturn when he left the Lake District in somewhat of a rush following the break-up of his marriage and he went to live in Billinge, a couple of hours South down the M6.

For a while he tried to rebuild his life down there, to get himself together, but it was very much of an uphill struggle for him and he found it hard to see light at the end of a dark tunnel.

It was obvious that he missed living at Bardsea on the South coast of the Lake District.

On occasions Annie and I called in to say hello to Erik as we headed down the motorway on our way to visit our daughter Katy at university, and we would stop and have a chat with him.

He tried to put on a brave front but we could tell, as could all his friends, that he had become deeply unhappy.

This was more than just a simple episode of unhappiness but was clearly becoming a serious, life-threatening disability.

Despite all this, when the subject of painting was brought up in conversation, his fire would be re-kindled and he would respond with fervour, vigorously discussing the merits of one artist or the technique of another.

From time to time Erik tried seriously to pull himself together, but it was a terrible struggle for him because, although one part of him definitely did want to survive, to get together, and to feel well, the other part of him could not even envisage the slightest success in these aims.

One day, after I'd not heard from him for a long time, I picked up the phone and told him that I was heading up to the Outer Hebrides for a ten day holiday on my own to do some painting, and I asked him if he would like to join me on the trip. There was room in my car and I planned to take an Island Hopscotch ticket from Oban and to head out on the Caledonian MacBrayne ferry to Barra, South Uist, North Uist, and Skye.

"No," he replied, "I've no interest in coming. You wouldn't want me as company anyway. I'm just awful to have around," and he continued in this manner for a while describing himself (but without using the exact words) as being in the depths of depression.

"Well," I continued, "I have the ticket for the car and myself and it would be a simple matter to add you as a passenger. I've never been to Barra or Uist, but I expect they'll be interesting scenically and I hope to get some painting done. You're most welcome to come too, and it may do you good, you know, the sea air, a change of scenery, getting away from the streets of Billinge. Give me a call after a day or two when you've had time to think about it a bit. Who knows – it could be good fun!"

I had begun to realise that his situation was really serious and that somehow he needed to be helped back into "the land of the living".

I hoped very much that he would join me, but more than half expected him to say no, or not to bother phoning.

So I was surprised and pleased when after a few days he called me and said that he would come.

A couple of weeks later and the two of us were boarding the red, white and black Calmac ferry at Oban and heading West through the Sound of Mull, being carried out into the Atlantic.

The chief steward's voice sounded over the ferry's tannoy inviting passengers to the ship's cafeteria to partake of herrings. He sounded for all the world like Gregor Fisher (alias Rab C. Nesbitt) as the voice of the Outer Hebrides Broadcasting Corporation!

Eventually Barra appeared as a small dot on the horizon. The dot enlarged, and at Castlebay we disembarked in the car and drove off to explore Barra.

The little island is easy to get around, being only about sixteen miles in circumference.

You can go round clockwise, or anticlockwise.

It was easy to find a B and B and we ensconced ourselves there for a few days, spending the days exploring the beaches.

I focussed on painting, and Erik on walking.

Each morning we would drive to a different spot and I would set up my easel.

His silent figure would head off across the silver sands, head down into the strong wind which prevailed at that time, leaving me to wrestle with my board and easel which were intent on taking off into the sky as if they were a kite.

"Barra"
from an oil painting by the author

Squalls of rain would intermittently lash down causing me to run for cover into the car, and the rainwater would mix with the oil paint on the board to form an emulsion which I would shift around with numb fingers and exasperation.

Almost as much paint got itself onto my anorak as onto the board!

The joys of painting!

Sometime in the afternoon Erik would reappear across the sands having walked all day – but we would both have things to report: he might have seen a flash of sunlight on a spit of land, and I took an interest in the sea birds and waders which were in abundance.

Then one day we were in the vicinity of the beach where the aeroplane, a twin otter, comes in to land on its twice-a-week scheduled flight from Glasgow.

The plane came in low over our heads, banked and turned in to land. Then it dropped, levelled out as it approached the beach, and made a landing on the silvery sands, then taxied to a standstill not far from us.

The tide was miles out and the beach was completely flat and empty, and this is the way they do it up in Barra!

Erik was delighted. It reminded him of the time he used to fly small planes and he began to tell me of his flying adventures. In fact he opened up about all sorts of adventures he had had, but it was obvious that flying had been something very significant for him earlier on.

After a few days on Barra we took the ferry up to Lochboisedale on South Uist and headed up the island, once again me painting and Erik walking.

This time I thought I would try some watercolours – my reasoning was that as there seemed to be so much water coming down from the heavens anyhow I thought it would mix better with watercolour paint than with oil paint.

I sat hunched over my board watching the heavy clouds and showers marching over the hills whilst Erik marched off into the distance over the beaches.

The weather remained showery and breezy but with bright periods, and the next couple of days took us farther up towards the tip of North Uist where we found excellent B & B accommodation.

Across the Sound we could see the hills of Harris glowing a variety of shades of blue as the clouds scudded over them.

The sea sparkled, and inland behind us the hills of North Uist glowered darkly over bright tarns.

Erik began sketching but was not satisfied with his efforts.

There was plenty of walking to be done.

One evening we were in the hotel in Lochmaddy having a meal and a beer. It was a Saturday night and the place was filling up with folk. There was a jukebox in the room and Erik put in some money and pressed some buttons and we listened as we ate. Then I got up

"North Uist"
(private collection)
from an oil painting by the author

and chose a favourite of mine, Bob Dylan, whose rasping voice grated out and mingled with the ever increasing ambient noise and clash of glasses as people piled three deep into the bar as if it were a rugby scrum and they were trying to push it over.

You could hardly hear yourself think, let alone Dylan complaining that he wasn't gonna work on Maggie's farm no more!

Erik winced, then went over to the jukebox again, put in another coin, pressed some more buttons, and came back with an intense look on his face; "Now just listen to this, John," he said, and so we sat there amongst the milling throng as some soundtracks from a Dire Straits selection floated into the room. For Erik this was akin to ecstasy.

You could hardly hear the music, so loud was the surrounding noise, but nonetheless when the track "Brothers in Arms" played I confess it sent tingles up my spine.

Later, as we drove back to the B & B, dark figures like zombies lurched from side to side in the road in front of our car headlights, weaving their unsteady way home.

The next day we bad goodbye to Lochmaddy and caught the ferry for Uig.

In front of us the Cuillin hills scraped the clouds as we approached thc Isle of Skye.

We visited Dunvegan, where I had once worked as a locum GP in my early days as a doctor.

Stopping at the Misty Isle Hotel, I recalled how Mrs Campbell's son, Big Rory, had been in charge of the hotel when I had stood in for the local GP, Dr Fisher, to give him a holiday, and how Rory had kept everybody entertained in the bar and, later each night, in the kitchen, singing songs, playing the accordion, and generally having a wild time. But this time the hotel seemed shabby and quiet. It had not been like that in 1974.

The weather was picking up and the Cuillins appeared over the horizon as we drove South out of Dunvegan.

We found a B & B in a remote spot somewhere to the West of Sligachan, and the next day I was keen to get Erik up into the hills.

"Tomorrow," I said, "let's go up to Coire Lagan. You're right up high there surrounded by big peaks and rock walls. It's a great place to be. Really impressive. You'll enjoy the walk and it's not so far."

Erik grunted assent, and so next day we set off walking uphill from Glenbrittle in hot sunshine. Our conversation as we went covered many things to do with art, and I remember telling Erik about the MOMA, the Museum Of Modern Art, which I had visited in New York not long before, and where I had seen famous works by Marcel Duchamp whose crazy constructions had caused consternation when originally exhibited, as they continued to do even now. There was the one with bits of string dropped onto a sheet of brown paper and entitled "Stoppages", obviously because their fall was stopped when they hit the paper!

I had found many of Duchamp's works intriguing and amusing, but I could not persuade Erik that they had any value.

I called to mind various other works of modern art and chatted away about their impact and curiosity, and how that differed from the classical and traditional style which was more to Erik's taste.

I remembered one painting by Christopher Wood entitled "Zebra and Parachute" which showed a sort of town centre scene with a zebra standing there disconsolately and the figure of a man dropping out of the sky on a parachute. Weird! Not even attractive, no bright colours, and somewhat childlike in its execution – but nonetheless evidently a "great" work of art, or else why would it be residing in one of the world's most prestigious galleries?

"Bloody hell, John!" said Erik. "How much further is this bloody lake? I need a fag!"

So we sat down in the sun while Erik smoked a cigarette.

We progressed up the hillside in this manner, stopping about every four or five hundred yards so that Erik could have a fag and moan about how far it was and how steep!

But the sun shone and we came eventually (after almost twenty stops and an entire packet of cigarettes!) to the smooth, flat boulders which lay gently baking in the sunshine on the shores of the little lochan which nestles in the heart of Coire Lagan.

Surrounding us were the towering walls of Sgurr Dearg, Sgurr

Mhic Choinnich, and Sgurr Sgumain.

The Great Stone Chute spread itself down the steep mountainside towards the lochan.

I could see the Sgumain Tower and pointed out to Erik the crack in which I remembered getting my helmet stuck as I had climbed the tower many years ago along with Bill McKerrow and David Nichols. I think I had got free by undoing the helmet strap and releasing my head, then struggling to wrench the helmet out of the crack.

We picnicked beside the loch and I went on up to the ridge beyond.

The day was hot, and the views from the top down over Loch Coruisk were dramatic.

Erik remained a tiny spec basking beside the emerald waters below.

He seemed more contented when I rejoined him. "Bloody hell, John," he said, "I don't know how you could walk up that far, and without stopping."

"Well," I replied, "If you just keep going slowly, slowly and take your time you can pace yourself so you don't run out of breath. But if you go too fast you tire and need to stop."

Erik had another cigarette and we walked down.

That evening he asked me how far we had walked.

"About four and a half miles," I replied.

"Bloody hell, John, that's a long way!" he said, "I haven't walked that far since I was a boy!"

Next day I suggested a walk to visit Loch Coruisk. We could take the trail from the Sligachan Hotel that leads all the way down Glen Sligachan and then over a low col and down to the loch, then come back the same way.

Coruisk is a fine, brooding, secret place in the very heart of the Cuillin mountains and I thought it would be a bit of a challenge for Erik, but the weather was beautiful and we could take all day. I thought he would feel good with himself getting to a remote lake set in impressive scenery.

"Bloody hell, John, how far's that?" Erik asked.

I glanced at the map; "About ten miles, maybe eleven," I replied, "but it's pretty flat – not steep like yesterday."

And so we set off.

The trail was perfect; virtually flat and easy to follow. Time slipped by as we chatted and walked, stopping every half mile for Erik to smoke.

The miles slipped past and after a bit I looked at the map and saw that we had walked about five miles and needed to head Southwest to cross a col before descending to Coruisk. Here the track began to ascend.

It was not long before Erik's voice came after me; "Bloody hell, John. How much further is it? I thought you said it was flat all the way. This isn't flat! It's bloody steep!" And then more ominously, "I hope this doesn't give me angina!"

"What do you mean – Angina?" I asked. I had not known about this.

"My doctor told me years ago I've got angina," explained Erik. "He said I wasn't to over exert myself."

"Bloody hell, Erik," I said, "It's a fine time to tell me you get angina now we're miles from anywhere. You'd better sit down and rest. How often do you get it? When does it come on?"

"Oh," he said, "I haven't had it for ages but I remember the doc saying I wasn't to do anything strenuous, and I told him not to worry 'cos I never do that!"

He sat down and lit up.

We progressed more slowly and thoughtfully uphill with stops every couple of hundred yards.

At last we crossed the col and began the descent to Loch Coruisk which lay below us. We reached its shore and both felt very pleased with ourselves having attained our objective. Erik was especially happy; he had walked miles further than he had ever done. He could not wait to get home and tell his nephew, who was at that time undergoing arduous selection for the Marines, and was still in the running after eighty-five out of the initial hundred applicants had been deselected.

"We made it," he said, grinning, "But I'm not going back up that bloody hill. Let's take an easier way back."

This was a problem.

"There is no easier way," I explained. "The way we came is the easiest. The only other way back involves heading South around the coast for a couple of miles on a more difficult track. At one point there's a wee bit of rock scrambling to get past a tricky bit. Then we'd have to get round to Camasunary and head North from there up to Glen Sligachan, and all the way back up the Glen."

"Bloody hell, John!"

But there was no persuading him to go back up to the col we had come over, so, after lunch and a long rest we set off on the coastal track.

The track winds up and down around the peninsula, with big, near vertical hillsides on the left, and the sea to the right.

The sun shone brightly and the views were superb.

We plodded along until we came to the "Bad Step" where you have to climb across the seaward side of a massive boulder. There are good foot and handholds, but for a few metres your heels are overhanging the seething foam of the Atlantic as it surges several feet below, and concentration is required to cross that bit.

"Bloody hell, John!" came the expected phrase.

"Bloody hell, Erik!" I replied, and then he was over the tricky bit and we were both laughing.

After that it was easier going, but I knew it was still a long way back to the car.

The afternoon passed pleasantly with frequent snacks and stops every few hundred yards for Erik to have a smoke.

We walked slowly.

We passed the bothy at Camasunary and then headed up along the bright waters of Loch na Creitheach with the craggy slopes of Bla Bheinn to our right.

The scenery was impressive indeed.

The sun was still high in the sky but most of the Northwest face of Bla Bheinn was in dark shadow.

Eventually we reached the point where we had left the Sligachan track several hours before, and we began the long, flat track back up the glen.

As we passed between the walls of Marsco to the East, and the massif of Sgurr nan Gillean across the valley, Erik declared he had much to tell his nephew when he got home.

He was beginning to feel mighty proud of himself, the distance he had covered and where he had got to, when suddenly the air above us was shattered by a deafening roar, and a Tornado jetfighter came in low round the corner of Bla Bheinn, skimming the surface of the loch below, and parting our hair as we stood there.

There is often a pursuit jet following behind, and indeed we saw its flash of silver as it hurled itself after the leader and in a trice it was over us and we felt the earth vibrate as the noise of its rockets slammed into the mountains around us.

Some people complain about low flying jets and the noise they make, but I can tell you that there is only one word for the feeling we had at that instant – Exhilarated!

"Yeeeeehaaah!" we shouted, and we danced around hopping from one leg to another.

That set Erik off in "pilot" mode, and he regaled me with his flying stories which kept us entertained all the way back to the car.

We got to the Sligachan Hotel in the late afternoon and decided to celebrate an excellent day's walk.

I went to the bar and ordered a pint each for us, but there was such a busy crowd and the queue was so long that I made it two each by the time I got our order in.

I carried the drinks across the room and set them on the table.

"How far have we been today?" he asked.

"Eighteen miles," I replied. "It's got to be about eighteen miles!"

"Bloody hell, John!" he beamed. "Eighteen miles!"

He could not believe what he had done. He was absolutely delighted.

He wanted to get home and tell his nephew all about it.

And so after supper that evening we hit the road South for Armadale and stopped for the night at a backpackers' hostel a few miles North of the ferry terminal.

Unfortunately the hostel had a bar, and Erik made for this with a determined look. After joining him for a beer I went up to bed in the dormitory, but Erik was clearly intent on more beer, so I left him downstairs.

I was woken up in the middle of the night by a loud crash as Erik fell headlong into the dormitory, landing on the floor. After several minutes he dragged himself into bed, evidently completely drunk.

The next morning I went down to breakfast and he joined me only a few minutes later. He behaved as if everything was normal, no headache, no hangover. He said he felt fine and I could not believe how that could be the case after he had had so much to drink the night before.

We caught the ferry to Mallaig.

I felt furious that he should have allowed himself to get so drunk.

In Mallaig we bought pounds of large, fresh prawns and cartons of orange juice and drove down the road till we got to Arisaig.

There we stopped at an inviting beach and decided to pull over and picnic on the sand. I got out a small camping table and two collapsible chairs from the car boot and we set them up on the hot sand by the water's edge.

As we sat tucking into prawns and orange juice we were surrounded by a flock of white geese that came looking for scraps, their long necks craning up at our table, making almost a surrealist picture of the scene.

Our meal over, I got out my paints and began an oil painting of the idyllic scene.

Erik lay down on the sand and fell instantly asleep in the sun.

It must have been quite a few hours later that I stopped concentrating on my painting and saw that the tide had come in so far that it was lapping at my feet. A cluster of holidaymakers was observing me from behind.

I had spent long enough and it was time to be on our way.

Erik was still sound asleep and I thought that the sleep would do him good, so I loaded up the car and eventually stirred him.

As we drove South to Glasgow he seemed more relaxed.

"Hey, John," he said, "I did the walk. Eighteen miles, was it?"

When we came to Glasgow we decided to visit the Kelvingrove Gallery. It houses one of the biggest collections of art in Britain.

We wandered around the pictures chatting and commenting, stopping now and again to focus on one which caught the eye.

"When going round art galleries," said Erik, "come away with just one or two pictures in your mind's eye. You cannot remember them all, so study just a small number carefully, and try to remember what it is about these that makes them so good."

We passed a picture by Christopher Wood, he of the 'Zebra And Parachute' at the New York MOMA. It was a harbour scene, thought to be of Mousehole or Newlyn in Cornwall. Its colours were somewhat drab and the harbour wall cut across the picture in an intrusive and obstructive manner. I was aware that Christopher Wood had died at a young age and had had an unhealthy obsession with drink and drugs.

We wandered around wrapped in our own thoughts. Erik disappeared from sight.

The next time I saw him was maybe twenty minutes later when I walked into one of the other rooms.

He was standing stock still, as if transfixed, gazing at Rembrandt's painting 'Man In Armour'. He stood like that for a long time, then he became aware that I was beside him.

"How does he do it?" he exclaimed. "Just look at that! He's got everything so subdued, all dark tones, all shadows and you can barely make out what it is – then Wham! He makes this single brush stroke of bright paint and there you have it – it's a man in a suit of armour. Genius!"

After several minutes of intense study he dragged himself away sighing and muttering, "How does he do it?!"

After that we went on to the Gallery of Modern Art in the city centre. Erik was not keen on modern art, I knew, but I had seen the gallery before and had found it immensely interesting and I wanted him to see some of the pictures.

On the ground floor he began to get enthusiastic and was amazed at some of the paintings there. Upstairs he was more critical.

Then something strange occurred; we were walking along a

corridor and there were several of John Bellany's paintings hanging on the walls on both sides, and Erik was turned the other way, and with his face in his hands.

He groaned.

"What on earth's the matter?" I asked.

"I can't take all this, John," he said. "I know what this guy means. I've seen it all before. Believe me, I really know what he's on about."

The pictures were large, loose watercolours painted by John Bellany as he lay in Addenbrookes Hospital, Cambridge, just after he had had his liver transplant. He was a talented and notorious Scottish artist and had been at death's door with liver failure due to alcoholism, when Professor Roy Calne had agreed to perform this life saving operation. The first thing that Bellany had asked for when he came round from the operation was paper and paints.

The nurses had brought these to him and he spent the next few weeks painting non-stop, lying in his bed at Addenbrookes.

The pictures were mainly self-portraits and were strikingly unusual in that they showed the artist lying ill at death's door in his hospital bed, with numerous tubes going everywhere.

Also depicted were the various doctors and nurses who looked after him, and there were a number of his earlier paintings, all dark, brooding, tormented, strange and rather frightening, showing people with distorted faces – not what you would call beautiful.

I told Erik how Professor Calne had come up to the Lake District and had given a talk and a slide show of his very own paintings, for he had himself been stirred by John Bellany into starting to do paintings of his patients, and he had delivered a moving description of his emotions whilst painting his various patients before they underwent liver transplant at his hand, some going on to survive and some not.

I pointed out to Erik that this artist, John Bellany, had, in this series of pictures, not only produced some of the most intriguing paintings ever done, in unusual circumstances, produced from his hospital bed, but also had influenced a great surgeon to take an interest in art and himself to become an accomplished artist.

Talking to Erik in this way he relaxed and was able to look at each picture and walk slowly up the corridor taking a more normal interest.

But I had never seen anyone so upset by a series of pictures.

We got back to Windermere later that day, and he drove on down to Billinge.

Soon after this I started work on a painting which I did very much in the hope that somehow it might influence Erik to recover.

I called it 'Artist Asleep On A Beach', and it was set, more or less, on the beach at Arisaig where he had fallen asleep.

I used big brushes, large tubes, and bright colours.

I tried to achieve an optimistic feel to the painting.

I used plenty of bold strokes of the brush, and I made the sunshine bright and the sea sparkling, and the sand warm and welcoming.

I took a long time with it.

It was not a simple landscape or portrait, but was done as a tribute to someone I liked enormously and who had himself such strong emotions concerning art, and it was in a way intended as a signal of hope, almost a talisman, that he would get out of his depression.

Hence the bright colours.

A small zebra floated cheerfully down on a parachute somewhere up in the clear, blue sky.

But the overall effect was, admittedly, enigmatic.

Over the next several months I saw little of Erik but was aware that he was still struggling with depression yet he had been willing to try different things, other than antidepressant medication, to see if they helped. He tried spending time at a place of retreat, and he visited a healer, but it all seemed to no avail.

In the summer of the year 2,000 I had an exhibition of paintings at the Steamboat Museum in Bowness-on-Windermere. The exhibition had been up for a month. There were fifty pictures and all of them had to be taken down because none had sold during the month of the exhibition.

I was feeling a bit morose about this as I began taking them all down and carrying them out to my car, when a young couple came in to the room and started to look at the pictures still up on the walls.

They instantly said they would like to buy the painting of the man lying on the beach. They said they were intrigued by it and asked me about it.

I said that it was a picture of a beach on the Scottish West coast and that the man lying there was a friend who had been troubled, depressed and unwell but that on the beach and in the painting, at least, he was at peace.

They said how much they liked it and they bought the picture and I confess I shed a tear as it went.

A week or two later the phone rang.

It was a police sergeant from Wigan.

He regretted to inform me that one Erik Gleave had been found dead at his home in Billinge, and had left a number of notes for friends, one being for myself.

The note explained Erik's decision to take his own life.

Somewhere there is a couple, whose names I do not know, who have, hanging on a wall, a picture painted not so much with paint as with emotion and hope.

And I did use a large brush.
